MW00511374

The Greatest Inning Ever Pitched.

By Richard Henneman

The Greatest Inning Ever Pitched
By Richard Henneman

Thanks to my family, former coaches, teammates, and friends. Much thanks to my sons and their teammates for taking on the challenges of sport and the lessens there in.

This is dedicated to the coaches that teach children to believe in themselves and the children who have guts enough to put on a uniform and see what happens.

Copyright © 2014 by Mark Minier & Broken Reed Books
http://brokenreedbooks.wix.com/reed
brokenreedbooks@gmail.com

Contents

Prologue

As a kid I loved the game of baseball. I played some form of the game, wiffleball, baseball, pickle, 500, home run derby, etc...., more days than not throughout the summer. If I did not participate in my favorite sport, it had more to do with the weather or a friend wanting to do something different than my preference. I have a wealth of my own sports memories, many of them are shared in these pages. And if you are like me, your life is full of your own fond recollections and also the privilege of watching new generations of young men build life-long memories on their own athletic journeys.

Life can also at times have a way of bringing controversy and challenges. Maybe there are others that have skated through life completely void of opposition, from a distance it can look that way, but I can only speak from the point of view of having grown up a little battle tested. We don't get to live our own lives from a distance, we have intimate knowledge of every hiccup and blemish that proceeds our successes. And if we are not careful, we can be misled by an illusion of not measuring up. I would say I too was on easy street most of the time, but every so often a road block would be in my way. I think controversy has a way of getting us to make up our mind about the things we are undecided about. I grew up with great freedom and great responsibility. Sometimes that freedom blew up in my face despite being generally uninterested in finding trouble, but I appreciate what I learned along the way, even if it was twenty-five years before the lesson was understood. I would say I have learned more in the desperation of struggle than the ease of success.

The story I am telling is from real events. I have re-told some of these stories over and over because it strengthens me and I like having the memory fresh. I hope when others hear the stories told, they don't hear boasting. Instead, I hope a clear picture of the fortitude we have within is exposed. We all have stories and these are my real stories, but I want for you to receive them as allegory to inspire inside you a sense of what is available when you give yourself, a friend or loved one a chance. Giving yourself a chance to succeed can sometimes be the bravest thing you ever do. In athletics, the office, or our hobbies, we practice to improve our skills. At some point, as we continue to work at it, it becomes second nature and we don't have to think about every move we make, even though we can still continue to learn and enhance our talents. We may even become exceptional at our craft, but some days we have a little something extra. The something extra can be written off or go unnoticed. But it can also be remembered and become fuel for keeping faith in times when we need a little light because our circumstances do not seem bright.

I have heard the term *'glory days'* in a neutral or even negative connotation. For me, having a few glory days to draw inspiration from has given me a push to keep going and a reminder to keep my chin up. The *glory days* I am referring to are not living off the memories of the past instead of participating in the present, rather, it is pulling the strength and inspiration of those few special moments of the something extra into where I am at right now. While my story centers around baseball and sports, it also tells of the overcoming virtue that is within all of us. This book is written from the position of someone working through and connecting the dots. Some of the chapters are written from my own challenges, of thresholds I have not yet crossed over but in time will. I would rather paint an honest picture that helps someone than a beautiful one that makes little impact. It is my hope that you enjoy my stories and find real substance and inspiration for yourself in these pages.

King of the Hill

Before I get to my baseball story, I want to tell you another story. I can remember a game that was played mostly by the boys at school during the winter months. I lived in southwest Michigan and we received lake effect snow every winter. This means that we were an ideal distance from Lake Michigan to get extra snow because it improved the conditions needed to make snow. Maybe it is just how memories from childhood work, but I remember three feet of snow being normal. And whenever the snow was plowed or shoveled into a mound, boys would be drawn to it for play. The game, king of the hill, was an every-man-for-himself battle to see who could ascend and stay at the top of the mound. If the pile of snow was large enough and there were sufficient challengers present, there would be several 'kings' contending to stay on top, while they pushed aside others trying to climb up the sides and gain the hilltop. When there were multiple 'kings,' they usually focused more on fending off others advancing up the side, but sometimes the excitement of being the lone representative at the peak would cause lateral challenges to be made.

I remember it being a very fun game that I played whenever there was a hill and someone to contend with. Because king of the hill was such a free-for-all, it was fun even for those that could not often keep their position on the top for long. And there was some order to it that made it bully free, because you had to climb the hill to be involved. You played if you wanted and knew what you were getting yourself into. At my elementary school, there was a very small hill for third grade students and a larger hill for fourth and fifth grade. If you climbed the hill to challenge for the top, you were fair game. If you stayed off the hill, you were left alone.

I have many memories of playing this game in grades 3-5. It was generally very good natured. It would at times bring out the competitiveness of the boys, but it had its built in way of settling things. I was especially good at it, and I admit that was a big reason I looked forward to playing during the winters of fourth and fifth grade. As a fourth grader, it was fun to challenge the older kids and beat them some of the time. I had to work my buns off to make it to the summit, but I was a force as I combined speed, strength and leverage. They would knock me off the top sometimes, but I was usually tough to get rid of once I made it there. As a fifth grader, I lived at the top.

Before I ever contended for the large hill, I learned to love the game on the third grade hill. Me and two or three of my best buddies played king of the hill on a pile of snow that was not even waist high to an adult. And there was really only room on top for one of us. But it was the traditional 3rd grade hill and we had a blast. Back then we all had one piece snowmobile suits and large, overly heavy boots. I think the epic moon boot fad came a year or two later. It was tough enough for a little squirt to climb in that gear without someone trying to push you down. But that was the fun of it all, it wasn't easy. My friends and I played on our little bump every recess. I remember how we laughed and screamed as we struggled for the top. It was a pretty even match and no one really cared about being on top, as much as we just liked playing. We were like happy, innocent, little puppies wrestling around.

The 3rd grade hill dynamic changed that year. It was a normal recess and my same group was performing our winter ritual, when an invader came to our spot. A fifth grader, who had actually been held back a year showed up. Because he was three years older, he was much, much larger than us. He would have been large even by his proper sixth grade standards, but he paid no mind to his disproportionate size, and he began tossing us off our hill. If he could have seen himself, he would have seen a ridiculous sight, this large boy standing on a little bump of snow, tall and proud. It goes without saying he had some kind of self-esteem and other issues that brought him to a hill of younger children. Maybe he felt ganged-up on at the bigger hill or maybe he just wanted to feel some semblance of success at a place he had spent one too many years. Regardless, he was out of his territory pushing around kids half his size. We left right away, and I remember feeling very dejected that day.

The next day, the three puppies went back to their play place and there was a repeat performance of the day before. We had fun until the larger boy showed up again and threw us around. We left to play elsewhere, immediately. This time it was obvious that the invasion was not a random occurrence, and I was really upset with the prospect of losing our hill altogether. I did not say anything to my teacher, but I was still thinking about it when I got home.

My dad could tell there was something on my mind that afternoon, and he asked what was up. As much as I wanted to hide my feelings, what I told him, I could not get out without crying a little. I had felt like something very important had been stolen from me. There was no gray area in this, the boy was not supposed to be there. This was the 3rd grade hill and me and my friends were the third graders. After I explained what happened, I felt relieved because my dad would tell the principal and get it straightened out for us. A light bulb was on in my head; if I explain my problems, a grownup can help.

I was shocked and frightened by my dad's response. "It's your hill. Take it back." Ugh, what part of the story of the mammoth 5th grader did I not say clearly? But that is where he left it, me against King Kong. And the funny thing about it was I agreed with part of what he said, it was our hill. We were the third graders. It is our hill! But I also understood my dad was crazy for suggesting we, or I, could take it back. I just wanted the boy to get bored of pushing us around.

One problem. It wasn't boring to him to push around some little kids and take what was theirs. It was his disturbed joy to do so. My friends and I faithfully showed up at our hill, and from out of nowhere, the goliath comes to steal another recess from us. He pushes us all from the hill and stands atop it. He is Attila the Hun. A proud, merciless emperor of the snow. And somehow at that moment, just before I turned to leave, tail between my legs, my father's words returned to me, "It's your hill. Take it back." In that instance, his words changed from crazy to powerful. What was impossible seemed right and possible. In that moment, I was overcome by the conviction to take back the hill from him and that it was my hill.

With this conviction, I charged up the hill and tackled him off. Then I gained the top before he could get his big body up there. Now I had leverage, and I knew what to do with leverage from wrestling with my dad. Before he always had the element of surprise, now I had the advantage and purpose to defend my position. I was not going to let him up. The other kids just watched as I successfully pushed him again and again off the hill. I had been intimidated before by his size and age, but there was none of that left. I knew what I had to do and I rebuffed him again and again. His courage was shrinking and after five or six defeats, he left. Forever. He never came back to our hill again. My friends and I played on that hill until the snow went away without being bothered ever again. I admit that I spent a little more time at the top after that day, but we were back to being innocent little puppies. The finality of overcoming that nuisance is what I take out of this. When I defended what was rightfully ours without doubt and reservation, I conclusively ended an invasion on our territory. I had the strength necessary to take care of our visitor and I am to this day, very grateful my father gave me the courage and opportunity to do it.

High School Baseball

I have played many sports, but baseball is the one I had passion about since I was old enough to swing a plastic bat. I loved hitting a ball and was forever looking for a wiffleball game with neighbor kids or a parent to pitch to me. I had an all-out swing and I just loved to mash the ball. Baseball was my number one during the summer, just ahead of fishing. Beginning at age seven, I would play baseball every year leading up to high school in a local baseball affiliation. Over the years, I developed a quite powerful arm, but my bat is what I would be known for through these early years. We did not have fences to drive the ball over where we played. I am glad, because it was fun racing around the bases. When the opposing coaches shifted their outfielders back, it just set a greater and more enticing challenge for me to bat the ball over their heads. My success in this summer pastime would progress me to my freshman year of high school at Wyoming Godwin Heights, fully confident of making the team.

Unless you consider throwing snowballs at trees conditioning for the sport, playing baseball in high school was the first time the sport had expanded from being a spring to mid-summer sport for me. The high school program started in March with conditioning and arm strengthening workouts. Practice moved outside in April. We played games through June for the school and following that season there was a summer league. I don't know when it became popular, but these days, fall ball is very popular and is available for all ages, but I don't remember it being an option when I played. Before my senior year, I worked on improving the drop on my split finger pitch with our catcher's coach, and that was it for fall workouts.

Freshman and sophomore years, I was in the starting rotation on the mound and split time at third base. As a kid, I definitely preferred batting to being in the field. I liked trying to knock the cover off the ball, besides, sometimes being in the field would last forever and you may not even touch the ball. When I reached high school, I greatly preferred the field. This was in part because I no longer lifted the ball over the heads of the outfielders every game, but also because I felt defense was a more intense source of competition, and I was evolving as a player.

Whenever I played, it was always exciting when the ball was ripped down the third baseline, but it became exhilarating as batters were able to drive the ball harder as we progressed from freshman to jv and finally to varsity. As long as I booted the ball only once, I had a chance to use my God-given, self-developed cannon for gunning down the runner at first. We had a very strong rotation at third, but I admittedly may have played more had I fielded a few more balls successfully the first time. I always had a good glove and kept most everything in front of me, but I think I did not develop as much composure as was necessary to handle the excitement of the ball coming my way. Pitching had it's own amazing intensity. This is a book about pitching, so I will focus on that throughout the rest of this story, but I loved playing the hot corner and will not forget the movement of the ball as it made it to you in an instant while arcing towards the foul line.

During these two years, freshman and sophomore years, I was by no means a dominant starter on the mound, but I was similar to the others in the rotation. I had a decent fastball and could throw strikes. I was composed enough not to have major meltdowns on the mound and was consistent from game to game. Where I was behind the curve, pun intended, I had no reliable secondary pitch. My curveball was garbage, and I had not learned any other option. My pickoff move started out scary, progressed to nothing special, but would develop into not too bad by the time I graduated. A more subtle nuance that I would develop later was pitching pace. It was helpful to have my best stuff when I pitched, but I did not know I may have had a part in extra errors and quieter bats when I was on the mound. It just seemed like a coincidence at the time. Later, I learned to work faster on the mound. It did not seem like much at first, but taking the extra three or four seconds out between pitches kept my fielders sharper and may have even helped our bats. When on the mound, you want run support and great defense. Working fast helps keep everyone tuned in. I had a moderately successful first two years as a high school pitcher. I was probably slightly above .500 to put a number to it, but I got by with arm strength and accuracy, and still had a lot more to learn to become a pitcher.

I performed fine those years, but I progressed a little slowly. My strengths increased some, but the areas of weakness did not develop. What it came down to was I had almost always progressed ahead of pace and took skill development as a natural cause of things. I did not know how to self evaluate, critique, and set goals that would make me a stronger player. This was not isolated to baseball; it was how I was. When I had a knack for something, I would practice over and over to improve, but

I did not look for, or was not often provided outside help beyond what I got from my dad or at practice. I had some talent, but I put a lot into sports too. However, I may have reached a plateau for a couple years because I needed to get some direction and work on some specific areas of my development. The coaches we had for ninth and tenth graders were good, but training pitchers was not necessarily their specialty. It takes a special gift and insight, and also time to give individual attention. That is not always available if there are not assistants to support the rest of the team's activities.

A brief aside... Besides having pitiful penmanship, another area that came easy to me was school. I was a very gifted student, and I always seemed to be able to understand and perform the lessons without much effort. I was an early reader, and writing, arithmetic and science were easy for me to learn. I really just had a desire to do well and as long as I had daily practice, until I mastered the unit, I was fine. I listened in class despite staring into space at times. I performed the tasks given and completed my homework. And that was a constant from elementary school through high school graduation. That didn't make me different. The unique part was that was enough.

As I progressed through the grades on into high school, obviously the classes got much harder. My sophomore year my mom, out of the blue, told me if I wanted to, I could be valedictorian, I barely knew what that was and had never considered it. It was quite surprising that my mom was thinking ahead to that. When she said that to me, I had not considered that I could do it. I was right among the leaders in GPA, but found myself with many excuses why I would not finish first. Mostly, I just thought very highly of the other students and did not put myself among them. I thought I would try real hard and come up short, so why try, right? I could list reasons why I thought each kid would finish ahead of me, but I could not come up with how I would finish ahead of them. When I thought about these other students, I took respect and mutated it into a level of intimidation. I was willing to not give myself a chance, and in essence would have quit before I ever got started.

My greatest fear was having to give something up. I played three sports and was active in many other school activities and friendships. Not that the other high GPA students weren't, but I struggled to give myself any credit at all. My mom said, 'Just put in a little extra effort and you can be valedictorian.' She made it seem realistic, and I agreed to go for it. She did not say I had to give up anything, she just told me to put in A effort. From that day forward it was now a goal, not an obsession, but something that would remain in my conscience. I had a shifting in thought and something to care about. I made sure I completed all my homework, asked a few more questions than I would have, studied a reasonable amount (not excessive) and just didn't give slack to any class. I would have finished high in my class, but because of that intervening talk from my mom, I finished first.

Varsity Baseball

At the end of my sophomore season of baseball I was told
that I was among a short list of players that may have the
chance to move up to varsity for the end of the regular
season and playoffs. A teammate, Sam, was up already,
but they were looking to add another player. They ended
up taking another pitcher/third baseman, Mike. I was
glad I was considered, but wanted the chance to play
more baseball for our school and to gain experience on the
next level. I had to wait until the following March.

When indoor pitchers and catchers practice began, I
worked hard in the drills and conditioning exercises. I was
now in one of the two older classes and knew that playing
varsity ball was probably the biggest stage I would get. We
did countless step-ups, running, throwing and stretching
exercises to make us better. Like everyone there, I pushed
myself very hard. When we got to pitching practice, there
was even more emphasis on a curve ball and mine just did
not break. Our skipper, Coach Stafford, worked with me
to try to get the ball to drop from the waist to below the
knees. He emphasized downward movement over
sideways movement, and most guys had a fair amount of

both. Whatever the reason, I just could not get there. When it did break, I did not have the control to rely on it in a game. My fastball was fine, but the deuce was just going to be a throw away pitch.

Besides working on a secondary pitch, Coach Stafford was cleaning up my pick-off move and stressing having a faster pace between pitches. Thankfully this was coming much easier. I now spun to my left like a cat, probably a slower, slightly less graceful one, and made accurate throws to first. I was not going to pick many guys off first, but I had a move that could legitimately keep runners close to the bag and not afford them a large running start on our catcher. Also, it was becoming clear to me through his constant reminders and repetition at practice how fast I could get to the mound, take the sign, and get into my delivery. It took a bit, but I now had an understanding of the concept of working faster and practical experience of being fast but not rushed. Coach Stafford even helped reduce extra motion in my delivery to help with accuracy and to continue to improve our catcher's chances of throwing out runners trying to steal. I was learning, but still limited to one good pitch.

Going back for a moment to the early days when one

pitch was enough, and I just had to be able to throw it over the plate. On one occasion before I could consistently throw strikes, we played a team that was coached to have discipline in a nuance that normally comes a little later. They were learning the art of getting a free base by, for lack of a better term, "taking one for the team." That is to say if the ball is pitched inside, let it hit you. Everyone has the goal to win, but especially with younger players, you primarily want to promote giving them an opportunity to develop their skills and confidence. I'm not sure if leaning in to get beaned is among the first lessons to be taught.

I was eight years old at the time. When I pitched, I may have thrown somewhat fast for my age, but at that age, I was still lobbing the ball. This early game stood out because I could not throw a strike to save my life, and what was more memorable, is all my pitches were inside. I hit batter after batter as they stood and allowed my inside pitches to hit them on the hip, arm or shoulder. I hit eleven or twelve batters in a row. I remember parents and coaches becoming vocal about getting me out of there. I could see in the kids eyes and posture they did not want to get hit, but their coach told them to crowd the plate and to take one for the team if I threw inside. I saw more than a few eyes well up with tears that were held back as I plunked these 7, 8, and 9 year old kids.

My father was the coach for our team and he did not think they should be given first base. Besides coaching, he umpired a lot and knew that the opposing batters were supposed to attempt to move out of the way if possible, and not stand there like statues. It is one thing for a couple kids not to move, but there was easily enough evidence to notice a trend. Considering the speed of the ball, it was no problem for them to avoid being hit and given my accuracy, still earn a walk. After debate, the umpire said they would not get a free base if they just stood there. I hit several more batters that were not awarded first base, and eventually got three outs because they were forced to swing the bat. None of the kids wanted to bat that day, especially after they were hit and were not given first base. For the other team, this may not have been the only game they were asked to take a ball in the ribs. It seems the emphasis on allowing the ball to drill them may have influenced their approach at the plate, because I cannot remember them making contact any other way.

This game was pretty much a fluke, I never had another

game like that. I credit my dad for waiting for me to get some outs before replacing me on the mound. He was very supportive of his players and spent what time he had between games to help us improve and be ready for our next opportunity. I worked through throwing inside by pitching batting practice while my dad emphasized giving the catcher's mitt my full concentration. I had been letting my gaze drift over to the batter, and therefore, threw the more than occasional bean ball. It was difficult, at first, to let go of my concern about the batter and only see the mitt, and then quickly bring everything back into focus after delivery so I was ready to play defense if needed.

My dad can be credited for developing my early pitching skills. I can remember pitching to my dad in the front yard of our home seemingly daily. I remember doing this for years. It took a while for me to become real accurate, but I remember throwing to my father over and over until it became very natural for me. After years of pitching to him, I was able to stop trying to get the ball to the glove and instead just deliver the ball, and it would end up where it was intended to. It became like breathing.

I point out the day I beaned the entire lineup in order to

say, even when you have talent, it is not necessarily immediately available. So much of the time it needs to be dug up. Some parts of my ability to pitch a baseball were buried pretty deep, but I worked at it and coaches and catchers spent time with me developing that skill. I may have had a gift to be able to throw hard and to a specific location, but it took a lot of practice and effort to bring it about. Each level of baseball I moved up, I had to grow into the position. I had to unearth a new ability to deliver the ball so it was not hit all over the place. To give a metaphor, a geode rock pretty well describes how we develop our talent. It initially is all within. There is promise and potential, yet we need to chisel away at it through training and experience, so more of the brilliance becomes visible and less of the old, gray outer-crust remains.

Junior Season

My junior year, I made the varsity team as expected, but I was still a little rough around the edges and without a curve ball. When the games began and the positions were announced, I was for the first time in my baseball life, not in the everyday mix. A similar thing happened in basketball a few months prior, but this was my sport, baseball. I began my junior year as a back up third baseman, behind Mike and Sam, and out of the pitching rotation. I felt a little left out, especially being off the pitching rotation or for that matter not being counted on to be a bullpen arm. Basically, I was on the roster but buried pretty deep. I did not see this coming, but I did not let being a reserve frustrate me or become an excuse not to compete. To keep it real, I do have a couple previous moments worth mentioning, where I did not show a lot of class, the first was a few years prior, but the second was only a couple months earlier.

I would say that throughout most of my childhood, I played sports because they were fun. I played for the love of the game. I liked to win, played to win, expected to win, but did not cry or throw a tantrum if my team did not win. Most of the time I enjoyed competing and playing a game. But I can also see a couple moments, in my teens, when I was too wrapped-up in the moment of a bad performance and disappointing defeat, and I showed bad sportsmanship and revealed a major lack of character. I will not just excuse the fits as a teen thing, because really it was a bit of a bad attitude that had crept in. I wish I could have shown more class and grace at times; unfortunately, I did not understand that as well as I do now, since I am learning that later in life. I will share two of my most memorable bad moments.

The first came during my final season of recreational baseball. It was the summer before my freshman year of high school. We were losing. Our team was playing bad. I can't remember how I was playing, probably either real bad or pretty good, because I was either mad at my team or myself that day. Somehow the performance really was getting under my skin. As the game went from bad to worse, so did my emotions. I was feeling embarrassed and ashamed to be part of such a bad performance. I don't know why, but we made uncharacteristically bad plays, and I somehow excused letting my emotions get away from me over a game. I was playing third base and eventually got to the point that I threw my glove. Either I made an error or somebody else did, but I gave my mitt a chuck. I did not slam it to the ground as a normal pouty ballplayer might. I gave it an epic hurl, sending it over the fence and against the front quarter-panel of a car. To this day I can remember the color of the car, yellow, but not the coupe de gras that got me to send my glove on a space mission. I had to hop the fence, give the lamest apology ever, and hop back over the fence. Then I had to assimilate myself back into a baseball game. The only saving grace here was the game was nearly finished. I am thinking we did not have much parental leadership with this team or I am just forgetting being majorly reprimanded. Regardless, it was a classless moment and very embarrassing to remember.

The second story is from basketball. I was a decent role player off the bench during my junior season of basketball, but nothing special. As a freshman and sophomore I split time on the low post, but by junior year everybody down low had outgrown me. I was still tenacious at defense and did a solid job rebounding the ball, despite my less than ideal size for the position. Even though my height was fully developed by now, my jump shot was not. I would get some meaningful minutes during many games while I gave a starter a breather, but it was during mop up duty that I would see extended action.

I may have been a little too motivated in these moments to prove my worth. One such game came when we were getting blown out of the gym by Forest Hills Northern. In the first half, I had been dunked on. Not directly, but Northern had ran an inbounds play and I tripped at half court, leaving their player with an open rim to jam the ball through. That didn't bother me too much. Maybe it should have, but my buddies afterwards just recommended I stay down next time instead of hustling and being posterized. As the game continued, our opponent stretched the lead, making it close to 30 points and it was time to, in coaches speak, 'call in the dogs.' Coach Carroll began to replace our starters little by little. I had made a couple baskets earlier and made a couple more with some extended playing time. I had nine points, which was not a lot for many, but for me it was a pretty special night. There was still about 4 minutes to go and coach called in the rest of the dogs. This meant some players, who almost never saw time on the court but were valuable practice players, got their turn.

It was tradition to get these players involved and let them take a majority of the shots down the stretch. Right away, myself and the one other holdover from the regular bench rotation, passed the ball to our teammates. The adrenaline of getting to play must have been overwhelming, because they were throwing up incredibly inaccurate shots, hitting the side of the basket and so forth, if they were even that close. It is painful to visualize these shots which were not indicative of their usual abilities. While this was going on, I was still trying to finish a basketball game and it was getting under my skin that they were just heaving the ball up without getting in a decent position and zero passes were being made. It was like being an unwilling member of the circus, being called the bearded lady and trying to convince everybody I was a dude. I already felt bad enough we were getting housed, and now we were getting clowned.

These guys worked their butts off as much as the rest of us, and this was their time to shine or something, but I began to feel embarrassed and like the game was being defiled or something. The bottom line is I must have been too proud of the way I played or lost my perspective for some other reason, because even though I knew this was precious little time that they would ever see during a game, I grew hot with anger and embarrassment. It was building with every uncoordinated heave of the ball. While I was an even headed guy in almost every situation, I did not deal with competing all out and feeling embarrassment well. Had I been off the court, I would have been fine. But I did not check my thoughts, and at the time, I wrongly considered what our bottom subs had done was desecrating to the game and our team.

The buzzer would finally sound and could have spared me any more embarrassment, but the main course was yet to be served. We shook hands and filed slowly into the visitor's locker room. Most of the players were in a much better mood by now. Even though we were beat badly, the reprieve did them well, especially with the comedy show that went on. There were three guys that never got to play except when there was a blowout. And there were probably only 3 or 4 blowouts. So basically, they ran all those sprints and practiced a whole season for maybe four chances to play. They were good guys to have around and I am sure for the moment, deservedly felt pretty good about being able to play. Nobody likes to lose, so I am sure they were not giddy, but that was not their fault, and they got the consolation prize of minutes played. While on the floor with them, I unfortunately took exception to two of the players.

What happened next is one of a few choice moments of

my life that I sincerely wish I could take back. I stole whatever joy they got out of that game. When I rounded the corner and got to the second row of lockers, I slammed a locker shut making a racket and yelled with all my anger the names of the two players and called them %$@ holes. Coach Carroll immediately spoke to me and got me to settle down bit by bit, while allowing the hurt I was feeling to come out in a less destructive way. He asked me to give an apology. I still felt, at the time, justified in my emotions because I had not yet regained my reasoning, and I gave a half-hearted confession, but they sincerely apologized to me and were more earnest about it. Wow, they actually apologized to me. I was caught off guard, and I still remember how their friendship and integrity in that moment genuinely touched me.

I lost it, and I was a creep that day. I had no right to act like that. Even if I was some great basketball player, which I wasn't, they did not deserve to hear the words I spoke in that tone. But the thing is, they did not do anything wrong. I did not see the situation for what it was and put my own personal achievements in front of my teammates. I don't tell this story to beat myself up, I know what I did was wrong and a failure of character on that day. Humans mess up sometimes and bigger humans forgive them. Now that I have grown, I think it is ok to share this in the context of this story.

Fortunately, this was junior year and would not be among my last basketball memories. Our senior year, Coach Carroll would lead us to become league, district and regional champs before losing in the state quarter finals. We became part of the school's and Coach Carroll's legacy. It was the second of his three runs to the quarter finals and having our achievements shown on banners in the school gym can be enjoyed and used as motivation by future student athletes.

Getting Some Help and a Chance

Coach Stafford gave me some opportunities now and then in the field or at the plate, but he held off from putting me on the mound. I still took bullpen sessions with a catcher but had not been called in for a varsity pitching appearance until we were well behind late in a game against a rival school, Byron Center. Leading up to this game, a former pitcher from our school, worked one-on-one mentoring me. These sessions gave me a little more polish and more confidence. Everything was just a little crisper and cleaner, and I was getting the maturity needed to take the mound at this level.

Back to Byron Center. I had been working in the bullpen with Lonny, the previously mentioned mentor, and was warmed up. When I finally was called into that game, it was in the middle of a Byron Center rally. Maybe coach Stafford thought there was no harm in putting me in because the game was out of hand and wanted to see how my sessions were going. Regardless of the reason, I was called in with a couple runners on and got out of the inning pretty clean. I started and pitched the next inning and slowed Byron Center down, giving up a couple runs total. I think Coach Stafford appreciated my ability to come into a bad game situation and go at batters. A reliever knows the odds are often stacked against them when they enter a ball game with runners on, but getting beyond the present conditions is part of the mental aspect of bullpen arms. Coming in to start an inning late in a game and walking away with the game held is the art of closing.

Soon after this game I was given another opportunity. Again the pitcher of record was struggling to get out of an inning, but this time the outcome was still in the balance. I finished the game, and we won. From that moment forward I seized a role. I became our team's closer. This was an awesome responsibility and a great job. I think I got the same excitement coming into a game with it on the line to start an inning as I did when it was in jeopardy because our pitcher could not get out of an inning. One situation was like being handed the keys to a shiny, new corvette and being asked to drive fast but not ding or scratch it, while the other was like being asked to pilot home a bomber that was shredded by anti-aircraft gunfire, the motor is still going, but getting to safety is a treacherous job. In these cases, I felt the same intensity as having a line drive come at me while playing the 'hot corner', except it lasted for minutes instead of a second or two. As the season progressed, it became a regular part of the game, to go to the bullpen in the late innings with one of my closest friends, Mark, and prepare for a relief appearance. Mark often entered the game when I did. He was excellent behind the plate and working together so much, we had a great connection. He called an outstanding game back there and was every bit a part of the save.

Once he decided to have me close games, Coach Stafford taught me a slider. He gave me a grip and a slightly different hand position and said throw the ball with your same fastball arm action. He had me work on it every practice, and it started to break. As it began to move more and more, he began calling for it in games and my slider began to produce strikes and outs. Before the end of the season, it was ridiculous. I really don't remember anyone touching it. I threw it at right-handers causing them to bail out or freeze before it broke over the plate for a strike. Other times, I started it over the plate and left them swinging at air. It was an out pitch. Over a few weeks I developed a secondary pitch that was dominating batters.

I now came in to pitch the last inning even when our

starter was fine. It was my job to make sure we won the game. Coach Stafford gave me the nickname, "Henneman," after the Tiger's impressive young closer at the time, Mike Henneman, and Sam came up with the line, "It all comes down to Hennie." This signified that the outcome of most games was decided under my watch. I was without a job to begin the season, but I stayed positive, listened and responded to every opportunity with 100% commitment. A pretty good formula when you think about it. Throughout the season when Sam or someone would call me by my new nickname or repeat the phrase, "It all comes down to Hennie," I was so honored. My opportunity came with mentoring, and I nailed it. As much as I wanted to bat more and play every inning, I would not have given up the experience I had to be a starter. The nickname stuck and so did the job of coming in to finish the work others started. I loved the new name and getting saves for our team.

Before the end of the season I had three pitches that I had complete command over: a fastball, a slider and a splitter. They were all excellent pitches that batters had a hard time hitting. Both the slider and splitter moved real late and the fastball had action, too. The split finger moved a good amount, but the slider moved as much as a big curve, but all at the end. It was a special pitch. It had a little something extra. Our bench got really excited when I came in, too. I held almost every game I came into, and finding the right role for me was awesome. As I settled into the position, everyone including myself, grew confident in my ability to pitch out of jams and save games. This was one of the few moments back then, that I had to wait and invest in something before there was a payoff, but the reward was beyond real.

It was a pretty magical season. We didn't have a slow start, but we definitely gained momentum through the season. Our pitching staff was primarily juniors, but we had some strong bats, good arms and fielders from our senior class. We battled every game and we made the playoffs. We hosted a very good Hamilton team in the first round of the district playoffs, and it was a pretty low scoring game. Each team put runners on, but the starters worked out of it before a rally was put together. It got to the 6th inning with us up a run and our pitcher tired. I warmed up in the bullpen before the inning started and came in with runners on. I got us out of the jam, and we came to bat the next inning with the lead intact.

When I returned to the mound, we had a two run lead. I

gave up an early hit and a walk and took a while to settle in and recompose myself. My stuff had been so consistent throughout the year and was still good, but maybe not dynamic because my accuracy was a little compromised. I would get an out, and then a second out with a runner on third and a tie ballgame. One of their strongest players and all-around athlete was next to come to the plate. I remember the pitch I threw him like it happened yesterday. I offered him a low and away, out of the strike zone slider, and he tracked the ball and lifted it just out of the reach of our first baseman's glove to win the ballgame for Hamilton. It was not a very powerful hit, but one he may remember to this day. It had a little less bite than normal, but that was the pitch I was trying to throw, and he hit it. This is the truth, sometimes the other team makes plays, too. It was a good game, and we lost. I would have liked to have had the stuff that could not be touched in the seventh and helped advance us to the next round, but we left feeling like warriors. Beaten warriors maybe but warriors. We had thrown our hat in the ring and competed.

Watching My Dad Run or Play Badminton

Ok, when I bring up competing, it is time to say a few words about my dad. I will keep it brief, but I could certainly go on and on. I have so many good memories with him, especially fishing the Flat River and bowling, which we always made into a friendly competition, and of course baseball. My dad, for the most part, was a very thoughtful dad that was engaging and generous with his time. He still is a pretty cool guy, but don't play him in badminton. Beneath his pleasant Saturday afternoon smile, jokes, and over a decade of toting an AARP card, lies a trained, shuttlecock smashing assassin that moves like a cheetah. He is, in a nut shell, one of the most competitive people I know. It is best to just talk him into volleying with you.

In March of 2012, I traveled to spend a weekend with him. On his schedule that weekend was a race. My dad is one of those guys that is all in when it comes to running. It is what he loves to do. Myself, I think the distances he runs are borderline too far to drive. This particular Saturday he ran a shorter race than he normally does, but it was bitter cold. I have not been to many road races, but I was glad I got to see this one, uh kind of. I relaxed in the school staying warm with the other few non-runners. As time began to get sort of close to when the runners might be back, I went out to the finish area.

Let me first describe what I saw as many of the other runners crossed the finish line. After the first dozen or two runners crossed the line full-bore, the vast majority of people were coming down the home stretch with a look of satisfaction. Many checked their watches to see how long it took them, but finished with beautiful expressions of joy. Other racers finished with friends and family members. They were not pushing to get across first but enjoying the moment of completing the race together. The end was the best part for them, and they savored it. As more racers came in, the reception, led by the MC calling out the times and giving congratulations, grew larger and louder. I really began to see the appeal and beauty of the sport. It looked like what community and family should be in the road racing context, giving support and cheer for the good someone has done or at least making it to the end. I was overcome by the affection that was shared as more runners were hugged at the end of their run than not. A smile crept on my face as I thought how fortunate I was to be my dad's family at this race.

Not to be overly dramatic, but I even saw a glimpse of heaven in this moment. I began to think, gosh, heaven would be like this, because it is not how you ran the race, it is all about crossing the finish line and the reception that follows. It is about hearing, 'Good job son,' and being welcomed home. So I was pretty taken by this metaphor and saw that regardless of the time it took to cross the finish line, in life or a road race for that matter, it is a cause to celebrate. It is about being welcomed into the presence of God, not stacking up the accomplishments on earth. The moment seemed to say, just gut this thing out if you have to and cross the line. You're welcomed in and all the rest is left behind. I loved it. I was having a much better time than I anticipated.

A little while passed and I see my dad. He is trucking down the home stretch as fast as he can. His strides are a little shortened by age, but he is pushing himself for all he has got. He checks his watch, no doubt to see how far off his personal best he will finish, and completes the job full-bore. He was not the only one to finish this way, but I remember him coaching me as a youngster before I ran one of, at most, a handful of races. He said to make sure you come burning through the finish line, which is sound advice for a competitor. So that's what I did, and he was there to greet me and tell me good job at the finish. On this day in March, I finally had an opportunity to pay him back, and he held true to his formula and he went full tilt through to the end. And not only through the finish line, but the hugs and affection, too. He burned right past it all and missed out, in my opinion, on the good stuff. It is worth reiterating that it was extremely cold, and I can appreciate 100% him needing to get into the building and let his body begin recovering where it was warm, especially since he runs in the grand master's division, 50 and up, and has been for more than 10 years. We did get to hang out inside, and I got over not being able to give him the reception I had planned.

My dad has accomplished much and has served many people, same as many men from his generation, no doubt because he pushes himself to the limit. It would be my joy to witness and share with him in more of these moments, and for him to experience joy without concern for performance, and to receive affection and to savor the finish. I hear about the friendships he has made through this pastime and realize that sometimes we anticipate an outcome and a circumstance can innocently cause our expectation to not be met for one reason or another. Next time, I will pick a warmer day to go watch him race.

Some of My Former Coaches

I had some great coaches throughout my youth in a variety of sports and I could share volumes about them. I am a youth coach myself, and part of the reason is because of the examples that were set before me. The coaches I had from middle school on up to varsity sports in high school were excellent. I have many incredible memories because of what they taught and how they joked around with us players. This section is just to highlight a few of the early baseball coaches who left their mark on my memory, one way or another.

My dad: It was already mentioned that my dad coached my baseball team. He was a great coach. He taught us the fundamentals of baseball and how to have fun playing it. I remember him giving his all to help every player reach his potential. He was committed to giving us every opportunity to learn the sport, and we practiced every weekday that we did not have a game. The thing about my dad was he chose to be totally vested in our team through the 5 or 6 years he coached and gave us a good foundation of skills to take on to the next level. We were a tightly knit group of players and many of us stuck with baseball and played together in high school. I would say my dad was a model of what can be accomplished through hard work, consistency and fun.

Coach Greg: As far as I know, he had no business coaching our baseball team. I say this slightly tongue in cheek but not really. Many coaches who volunteer get involved when their children are playing the sport. Coach Greg did not have a kid on the team, but maybe for sake of argument, he may have wanted to get some experience before coaching his own kids, who were quite small at the time. A pretty solid idea if true. I wish I would have opted to gain some experience before taking the helm as the parent/coach for my children.

Coach Greg was kind of a mystery guy. I figure when my dad stopped coaching, someone dug this guy up from who knows where. I almost imagine him being recruited to coach over a hot dog and root beer. Maybe he lost a bet. I don't know how he got involved, but he coached us for two years. It was a major culture shock, partly because it was somebody new, and largely because he was a complete opposite from what we were used to. Coach Greg was not impressively organized. He may have liked baseball but did not show that he had an inherent understanding of the details of the game. He was just some random guy, that was a mechanic out of his front yard, that frankly did not know that much about running practices. To his great credit he was willing, and I think that speaks volumes. And maybe some coaches are born, but the rest of us have to learn on-the-job. He was blessed with a talented team of experienced players. I do, however, think he missed his calling and should have been cast as the new coach for the Bad News Bears, a popular movie around that time, because he had a hilarious personality and frankly would have been better for television than coaching actual kids.

I can form memories of him hitting balls to us and pitching batting practice. And I remember he brought in one of his friends or colleagues to help us to be more successful at the plate, and the friend's contribution was to teach us to tap the bat and spit on the plate.

Maybe there was some solid teaching going on but we just remember all the quirky stuff from childhood, because the rest of it, more or less, blends together. I don't even remember any games from the two seasons he coached us, just a glimpse here and there of practice. Honestly, I mostly remember my friend John and I going to Coach Greg's house after school because he lived near our middle school. He had four or fives cars in his large front yard.

My favorite was a yellow Fiat that didn't run, and he called it a 'fi-fart.' He would work on his cars, be occasionally joined by his two little grubby kids and called in for dinner by his wife. I remember the whole family had a grubby, or a little shabby look to them, and at the same time his wife and children were beautiful. The funny thing about this guy was he was unexpectedly kind to my friend and I, and extremely loving and sweet to his two small children and wife. He had a fantastic personality and liked sharing what knowledge he could. As much of a clown he happened to be with the baseball team, he was one of the more sincere and affectionate fathers and husbands I remember from my youth. It is so easy to picture his gentleness with his family.

Coach John: Coach John was a card. I think he coached because he loved baseball and liked to be a part of it. I do not ever remember seeing him without a Chicago Cubs hat or jacket on. In fact, I know I never did, because he wore them all the time. He never really got too involved with the team, but by now we were eighth and ninth graders, so he could get away with being a little lax. Besides, he had great players on his team, especially his son. I could say he was not likely too responsible for developing that talent based on what I saw. But there was no denying his son was a fantastic athlete, so there must have been much more I didn't see, especially when he was younger.

What I can say about Coach John was that he loved the game and presented himself to be more of a fan of baseball, but it is possible he may have also been a strategic mind of the game. He probably did work with his son since the cradle. I don't doubt it at all. He was an intense fan of the Cubs and a loving, supporting father. Besides the first week, we never practiced, and I think we were fine with it because we were eighth and ninth graders and everyone had more to do by then. Coach John gave the lineups before the game and that was the apex of his job. We had more freedom and responsibility than we would ever experience on a team, but it worked. We had a stacked lineup, so we bashed the ball around and then went across the street for ice cream afterwards. We were older and much more social, and our parents let us hang out at the parlor for a while after the games, which made it a fun year. Did I mention Coach John was a Cubs fan?

Me as a coach: I am a volunteer youth basketball coach through the YMCA and some day may be reflected on as well. Hopefully not for all the mistakes I have made. Us dads coach because we love to share the things we know and love, and it is a privilege to pass on the positive lessons from our own childhoods. Most every child that is exposed to athletics loves it, and being a small part of that joy is the best thing since sliced bread or the advent of the 3 point line. Through the YMCA, we have gym time enough for an hour of practice and a game per week. Every sport I ever played, we practiced every day for at least a couple weeks, and then continued to practice every night during the week when not scheduled to play a game. My norm as a player is very different to my norm as a coach. I always have so much I want to share and yet only one day of teaching before sending them into the arena to play a game. It is a little contrary to my personal grid, but then we grew up with fewer options to divide our time.

Regardless of the speaking, teaching or coaching engagement, I am not the type to finish before my time is up very often, if ever. Because of the time constraint with my basketball teams, I tend to get right down to business and sometimes fret over what is not accomplished. I admittedly want to get them from A to Z a little too quickly at times and can try to pack 7 pounds of basketball into a 5 pound bag. Besides monitoring the amount of skills I teach per session, I admittedly need to learn how to clown it up a little more so the kids I coach have a little spice in their memories, too. If my memories are any indication, humor and friendships are the most sustainable to the tests of time.

Over the years, I have been able to learn on the job and grow into the position. It has not been a super easy process. I thought coaching would be a lot simpler given my background, but I have had to accept that I too was a work-in-progress, and toughed it out. One fundamental I have had to learn is to teach everything and not make too many assumptions. And at the same time to be patient and cover what I can in practice and accept that you just can't get everything in you want to. I wish I could say this has gotten much easier at the time of this writing, but I think it is, to a degree, the nature of things.

One of the bigger mistakes I have made is not understanding all the differences in kids and showing them complete respect even while trying to help them grow. I am learning they all have very different personalities and that is a good thing. Unfortunately, I have misunderstood them and some of their shenanigans at times and not been as supportive and respectful as I should have been. That is a bitter pill to swallow. Besides just having unique mannerisms and ways of responding, different things come easy to the kids and they all learn and listen in different ways. I thought when it came to sports, children would be more similar, but they are all very unique individuals who have their own home environments, experiences, priorities and readiness to show their capabilities.

Coaching has also been very rewarding for me personally. Sometimes it is seeing a kid improve or gain coordination he didn't have a week ago. Other times, it is watching our team close the gap a little on some very good competition. But a lot of the time it is just looking at your group and seeing that they are having fun. Seeing in their eyes, they will be back for more next week and keep on playing the game after the season is over. Sometimes, however, it is within myself. Learning to instruct a kid with a personality new to me with respect takes growth. Learning when to be real sensitive and when to be a little tougher takes growth. Knowing which plans to stick to and which ones to drop and move on from takes growth. Remembering to take a moment and listen to the story he or she wants to tell you takes growth. And giving compliments individually to let them know that you see how well they are improving or at least trying takes a little growth, too.

I admittedly am not, at the moment, a Wooden or Izzo clone; in fact, I am not sure how I would grade out against my volunteer peers, but like my teams, I'm improving one practice or game at a time and having fun learning.

I have so many memories of very good coaches that I played for and only a few that may have needed some seasoning. I have had to accept that I started out needing seasoning, and I would not immediately be like those coaches I give high regard to, locked away in my memories. I look forward to more opportunities to see how much I can grow and how much fun I can have being a youth sports mentor. It's been my great privilege to be involved and being around the kids is a lot of fun. As a father, I am so thankful for the other men and women who have stepped up and volunteered to coach my sons as leaders of teams of their own or on the sidelines with me. It has also been enjoyable to begin to associate with the opposing coaches in the league because during the game, it is all about learning, fun and competition. After the game, it is about friendship and community.

The handshake can be the best part of the competition

when two teams have given their all during the game and in the end extend their respect and gratitude as they extend their hand. In my life, playing pickup basketball has been the greatest teacher of this. The gym I play at, has a melting pot of men who come up to compete at a game they love. The court is generally comprised of players a decade or two younger than myself, but there are others on the north side of 40, same as me. The teams assemble, more or less, on a first come, first serve basis and you play with different guys every time you go to the gym. If you win, you stay on; so besides the sweet taste of victory, there is another great incentive to win, especially when the gym is full of guys waiting to play.

Part of the magic of pickup ball is learning to react to a random cast of players so that in that moment you are a team. You learn how the others play and assert yourself and your style of play into the mix. There is something cool about making a cut trusting the pass will be there, and having it threaded through a needle from a guy you don't even know. There is a special bond in sports where players make connections on a unique level. Even the men on the opposing team are part of the bond. You lock horns with them and give everything to beat them, and in the moment the winning basket goes in, you share with them the gratitude you feel for giving you a challenge. In this moment, winning has shifted from the ultimate goal to secondary and when pickup ball is at it's purest, you feel a real thankfulness for having the opportunity to play, regardless of whether you won or lost. Maybe this dynamic exists because of how the teams assemble and there is no guarantee of having enough players, much less who will be on your team. One minute you are rivals and the next teammates, fighting together to stay on the court. I think there is a lot to be learned from that example.

Versus Lee

This game I am going to share about is easily the most memorable game of my sports career. I can remember big hits and glimpses of plays here and there, and what it felt like to gun a guy down from third base, which I can sum up in one word, awesome. I remember the highlights of my sporting days, of this particular game I retain very vivid memories, especially of one particular inning. But besides this game, I mostly remember bits and pieces.

It was the spring of my senior year of high school and still in the month of April. We had played less than a handful of games and, we were yet to be in mid-season form. The day was crisp and we traveled to nearby Kimble Stadium to play a league game against Godfrey-Lee High School. They were not a major rival because although they gave their all and generally kept it close, we almost always found a way to beat them regardless of the sport. The school was by far the smallest in our conference by population. They always had some real good athletes, were well coached and very competitive, but we seemed to have their number. Playing at Kimble Stadium made the game a little extra special. Our home field was usually the nicest venue we would experience, but Kimble was a small college field that had it's own amenities and charm.

Our ace pitcher, Sam, was on the hill for us. He seldom gave up more than two or three runs, so we figured to win with a little run production. Unfortunately, as the game progressed, we were not able to capitalize on opportunities to open up the game with key hits. We drove in two runs to their early one run, but we were not able to extend the lead beyond that. Our bats were alive, but we hit balls at defenders or had an untimely strikeout that kept us from stringing enough hits together. We frequently threatened and were retired without a run while they were counted out in order after Sam settled in and took command of the game. He wasted little time between pitches and with all his pitches working, he made his performance look effortless. This day, he relied mostly on his fastball. If the batter did not strike out, it was a lazy fly ball, and if not a fly, is was a grounder directly at an infielder. He was putting together a nearly flawless performance, and he kept the game moving.

The confidence level was right at the line of maximum confidence without going overboard. Our dugout was lively with excitement and chatter. Nobody made any assumptions, but it felt like we could break this game open at any time, and if not, we were secure having only a one run lead. It was rare to be this settled under the circumstances, but that is how dominating our star was playing. Sam was a mentally strong and gifted pitcher who relied on accuracy and ball movement to retire batters. On this day I was enjoying seeing him pitch with even more accuracy than normal, locating the baseball on the corners, above the letters, or at the knees for swinging third strikes.

Besides having an ace on the mound, we had a stout defense. The infield as a whole was excellent. Each position had a player that had range, fielded well and threw accurately. And our outfield was pretty much the same way. Everyone had enough range to get to balls and make plays. Most of the time we were efficient and did not give opposing teams many extra at bats.

The 6th

Fast forward to the bottom of the sixth inning. As mentioned before, it has been a close, low scoring game. We are leading 2 to 1, and even though I would normally come in to close out a game in the seventh, I was thinking, 'not today.' Sam, our ace starter is on the mound and he is pitching a gem. Lee got a run on us early in the game, but Sam is really in charge now. He rolled through the middle innings and I can still see his confident jog off the pitcher's mound, each time he retired the side 1-2-3. All his pitches were working, and his pitch count was low. I cannot remember another time when a dugout was so relaxed for a one run game. We were loose and confident, and I was just a spectator, watching a great performance.

Sam took his warm up throws for the bottom of the sixth inning, as we looked on. From the dugout, we anticipated another quick half of an inning. The home plate umpire called for the batter and the bottom half of the 6th inning began. Sam took his windup and proceeded to throw a first pitch ball. And then he went through his motion again and threw a second ball. He walked the first batter of the sixth on four straight pitches. Ok, whatever. It seemed unexpected, but maybe he had a reason for pitching around him. Sam followed that up by matching it. A second straight walk. Eight pitches. Eight balls. It was unusual, but I remember thinking, 'eh, he is trying to be a little too fine.' 'Too fine' means that the pitcher is concentrating on throwing the perfect pitch on the black corner of the plate or right at the knees rather than giving himself a little margin and making sure he throws a strike. It is akin to trying too hard. Many times the situation does not call for the perfect pitch and being 'too fine' is an aspect of being overly cautious about a certain batter and is a negative condition in the mental part of the game. It can be overcome if caught and a mental shift is made.

In this case it was a symptom of Sam being able to pick his spots over the last five innings, because he had been surgically accurate. Now, he is trying too hard to paint the corners, but one good pitch and he is back on track. Nobody flinched. Sam will be alright. Next batter, and the next pitch is another ball. Alarms start going off in all our heads. Coach Stafford calls out to him and motions for him to settle down. To take his time. Sam steps off. Relaxes. Loosens his shoulders and takes a deep breath. He positions his right foot along side the rubber and looks in to the catcher for the sign. He nods his head that he has it, glances back at the runner at second and returns his gaze to the catcher's mitt. Sam takes one more deep breath, lifts his left leg and delivers it. Another ball.

"Hennie get ready. You're going in," commands Coach Stafford. "Time!" he calls to the home plate umpire and begins slowly making his way to the mound as Derrick, our junior catcher and I simultaneously dash out from the dugout to the adjacent bullpen. As we go, Coach Glusa, our second assistant coach says to hurry up. That didn't mean he had a short attention span and forgot we were just sent out, but it meant get as many throws as you can in before the ship takes on too much water. It was crystal clear enough in the span of ten pitches, that whatever Sam had going for him was lost and he could not get himself and the team to dry land. I threw the ball to Derrick five times, increasing the velocity with each delivery. I pointed with my glove for him to take a catchers stance, and as I did, my eye caught the assistant communicating to me again by motioning his right hand in a quick revolving motion, signaling to get ready fast. I nodded understanding, as I stepped forward and threw my first warm up pitch. After I let loose my second warm up, I looked over and gave Coach Glusa the 'I'm ready' nod. He immediately relayed the info to our head coach.

I gave him the sign a little early, because I knew I would be able to squeeze in some more throws. I was very confident in myself and felt I was an expert at getting ready under stress, even though for the record I recommend making sure you get in more throws. Once I was in the bullpen I had no clue of what was going on in the game because I had a job to get ready to do. I fell out of touch with how the inning was progressing, but from the body language I was reading from everyone, it was not improving.

Coach Stafford called for time. Now, for the second time in the inning he made a visit to the mound, Sam would have to leave the game, and I would take his place, but not before I would get three more throws in to Derrick. Jogging to the mound I could feel my excitement rise and I could see there was a runner on each bag, and Lee's bench was considerably more lively. Coach Stafford gave me the ball and the run down. "The score is 2 to 1 still. Sam has walked the bases loaded, and there are two balls on the batter at the plate. There are no outs." I can take a scan of my life from a child till now and find many times when I have felt like a situation was this dire. The bases of life have often been jammed with no outs. And yet, somehow I got through it. I think most adults can relate. But this was actual bases loaded with no outs. And what made it more vaunting is Sam had already thrown two balls to the next batter. I had a special role with our team, but this was beyond the call of duty. Never the less, I soaked that info in as I was given more warm up pitches from the mound. Sam had thrown 14 straight balls and the batters from Lee had the take sign, which meant they were not going to help me out. It would be up to me to throw a strike and right away because there was no margin. I was given a generous six pitches from the mound before the ump called for the game to start.

My mind was racing. I had only 16 total throws, and only the last few was I cutting it loose at full speed. All of them had crossed the plate above the letters. The game was starting, and I was not sure where the ball was going. My release point felt a little early, but more than that I was a ball of nerves. In my mind I knew the circumstance and could not avoid thinking it was hopeless, regardless of how veteran I was at being put into these situations. The part of the whole deal that was the toughest, was we were still ahead. Even though the runs on base would be credited to Sam, they had not yet scored and it was me that would ultimately fail the team. Excuses and reasons for losing the lead were winding their way through my mind. My goal, as it was beginning to form in my panicking brain, was to get out of the inning tied if I could pull off a miracle, but realistically I just wanted to keep it close. We still had another at bat.

Now for our brief committee meeting before I would play Daniel in the Lion's Den or those funny named guys that were thrown into the fiery furnace; somebody, somebody and Abednego. Besides myself, the conference at the mound included Mark, my long-time friend and bullpen catcher, Mike our third basemen, Eric our short-stop, Germaine our first basemen and Coach Stafford. Mark retrieved the ball from his catcher's mitt and placed it into my glove. Coach looked at me with a bright, almost professional smile that I still can visualize in my mind, and said, "Don't worry about outs. Let's just see if you can get one over first." And then he even chuckled a little. He spoke in such an easy way, like he forgot what the heck I was coming into. How could he be so peaceful? Well, it wasn't him that would be pitching. Then it sunk in a little. 'Let's just see if you can get one over.' He knows I have done nothing to earn this mess. He knows I could not possibly be prepared well enough to take on this Goliath of a circumstance. On a good day with full warm ups maybe I had a small chance, but I had only a few tosses, and it was a cool April day. That means I had a less than 0.0 probability of holding the lead.

But he isn't asking me to be the hero. He only asked me to see if I could throw a strike. I can't fathom how, but maybe he has been around baseball long enough to know anything is possible, and he trusts and believes in me. Adrenaline was firing through my veins not confidence, but I forgot about getting an out at that moment and considered that I might be able to throw a strike. Left alone and waiting for the game to resume, I stepped onto the rubber from the back of the mound. With bases loaded you don't have to hold the runners, so I prepared to throw from a full windup and looked in for the sign.

My junior year I would have pitched from the stretch. Left side to the batter, right foot along the pitching rubber length-wise. A more concise pitching motion. Often times I came in with runners on and it allowed me to concentrate on developing one type of delivery. Today it seemed right and I felt more comfortable, to have the extra movement of rocking back and going through a full windup. In hopes of settling my nerves, I would use this extra movement to prolong the moment of release.

Another Story Involving Sam

I have had many years to reflect on this game. Before going forward with what happens when the umpire calls 'batter up' to restart the game, let me take you back to another time Sam would get me into a 'fiery furnace' type of scenario. We grew up in nearby neighborhoods, played on the same and later rival little league teams. Not the actual Little League, but what was derogatorily referred to us by our freshmen coach as 'rocket league.' That comment was fuel to an already confident group that made up 75% of the team and the entire pitching staff. Sam and I also went to the same elementary school.

School was where Sam would bring controversy to my door step. As I said before, I had to go through some rough times and trouble every so often would come find me, since I had an extreme habit of trying not to find it. Sam, probably since birth, loved two things passionately, sports and a good fight. He was scrappy, just like the character that was added to the show Scooby Doo. If it was a slow day on the play ground, he knew how to get some action. He was a miniature Don King, except Sam was game to scrap, too. No fights? I'll arrange one. There was another kid, a real tough kid I'll call Fred. Fred was the kid at school with the reputation, the ability, and track record of backing it up. He was one of the biggest kids in our 5th grade class and would fight anyone, anytime. If Fred was the heavyweight champ, I was big and thus, in his same weight class and Sam was ready for the main event. As much as I had to defend myself over the years, I never was interested in fighting and would avoid every confrontation I could.

But like it or not, I was the number one contender and Little Don, decided it was time for Fred to defend his title. The day it would take place was a cold winter day before the snow came that year and lunch recess was wrapping up. I forget what I was playing, but I was a little slow to go in from recess and as I was about to return to class, a mob of 11 boys stood in my way. The fight card must have been drawn up long before I knew about it, because it was well organized. Many of the boys were guys I played with, but not today. This was not play. Sam called out the challenge and Fred readied his fists. 'I am a dead man,' went through my mind. And 'this is going to hurt,' went through my body. I either get beat up by Fred or if I start to win, the rest will jump me.

My fight or flight instinct kicked in and I ran for it. The

group of them pursued. I ran and I ran, still they always managed to block me from making it into the building. I could hear them at times call out to me as I dodged this way and that. So I kept running and eluding the mob. I was pretty fast, but it, in a funny way, almost seems like there was an odd, almost mature order they were following, one that makes Kimble Field seem less like a coincidence. The order was, 'Let him run until he decides to turn and fight.' I did not know it yet, but I had to confront Fred. Evidently, I had a lot of stamina and so did the mob, because I ran for a very long time. As I began to tire slightly, I went all out for the northeast door. It was locked. No entry. There was only one way to safety, through Fred and the mob. It amazes me to think that we were not looked for by our teachers. A different time all together, I guess.

Ok. This is it I decide. My worst fear by now is not battling Fred, but having to fight them all. I decided that if I would have to fight them all, I needed to have the strength to do so. There was no point in running anymore. I stopped and turned towards Fred and Sam. The rest of the boys filled in to form a circle. It sounds cliché, but they did. There was excitement in all of them, but something else in Sam as he said something to the effect of, "Let's get it on!"

I brought myself somewhat upright, with bent knees, waist and raised hands. The champ tightened his fists, his smirk slipped off to a growl and his ice blue eyes burned with fire. He bounced toward me as the aggressor. I stood my ground not giving in to the fear that wanted to control me. The moment before he strikes, I step into him, locking my grip securely on him. He does the same. There was a moment of struggle as the heavyweights engaged not as boxers but wrestlers. There might be some face pounding yet, but this altercation was going to start out as a battle of strength and leverage.

I had gone into the fight afraid. Despite all my scrapes with rough kids, I had never punched someone. Besides, I was well aware of Fred's earned reputation. I knew it was not all hype, even though Don King was good at what he did too. But deciding to fight was a resolute thing that came with courage. I would worry about the next guy if I got through my first battle. But now, with locked arms, I was committed to see this thing through. I hung in long enough for my nerves to subside, and as we pressed and pulled, I realized something. I knew leverage was something I was good at, but I was stronger too.

The second I knew it, I tackled Fred to the ground, pinning his arms to his chest with his back to the pavement. The circle of boys stayed put. After a lengthy pause to let the moment settle in, I asked Fred, "Are we done?" He replied, a little weakly, "Yeah." I cautiously got up and began taking a couple steps away when he sprung up like nothing had happened and came after me again. I was not caught off guard by this. Still in the circle, I turned to meet him again. This time there would not be a struggle as we locked arms. I put a little something extra in it and I slammed Fred to the ground, showing him the full extent of my strength. I held nothing back. I said with conviction, "We're done," and I got up and walked toward the school never looking back. The circle of awed boys opened up. The challenger had won in two rounds. I don't know what went on after I left, only that I caught a very satisfied look on Sam's face as I passed him by.

I would much later speculate that he probably did not come there to get me hurt, but to get me to fight. To get me to confront fear, and he wanted to see a battle too; let's not kid anyone. I don't condone looking for fights, especially as a father of two young boys, but I realize that you can only run from trouble for so long. And then it is time to stand your ground. You do need to be able to confront the things that rise up. Life, my life anyway, has had a way of bringing real challenges my way until I am ready to meet them. I seem to completely forget how to fight in between those moments of standing my ground. It is only when forced, that my will and strength of character rises and overcomes. The key to not being intimidated, is to not worry about all the battles you may have to face, but to face the battle you cannot avoid at the moment. The one you are already in, like it or not.

The Save

So back to the game versus Lee, the sliver of hope coach
gave me was sinking into my mind. I might be able to
throw a strike. Maybe I can do that much. He has me
focusing on just this first pitch. I am thinking to myself,
ok, I know I am nervous. I am extremely juiced and I have
been letting go an instant early. 'Finish your pitch,' I
dialogue to myself. I should have been dialoguing, 'Get a
hold of yourself,' or 'Chill out man!'

The catcher, Mark and I have worked together a lot. He
calls such a good game behind the plate, asking for the ball
in a specific location, and I normally deliver on cue. We
have chemistry. The ump shows with his hands two balls,
no strikes and calls, "Batter up!" This snaps everyone to
attention bringing us all into the moment and spurs some
chatter from the opposing dugout. It's on!

The batter is in his stance and I am left toes and right
heal directly on the rubber, ready to go. I am breathing,
slow in and then all the way out, gathering myself. I bend
forward and I look in for the sign, focusing on the call.
Our catcher Mark, understanding the circumstance, does
not conceal the sign under his bottom, disguising it from

the batter. He holds it straight down, one finger, for anyone to see. Fastball. He pulls his glove up and holds it waist high, center of the plate. This all means, 'Nothing cute. Throw a strike.' This deliberateness further sinks home the simplicity of my job. Mark has just reminded me of the message Coach Stafford spoke, 'Just try to throw one over.' Like the days in the front yard with my dad trying to master throwing strikes, I just want to groove this pitch right into the mitt.

The thoughts in my head go something like, "Ok. I don't know where it will end up, but I'm going for it." Now I gave myself a chance. I would be brave enough to throw a pitch with no fear of what would happen. The moment was here, so I silenced the Times Square like billboard of negative messaging trying to own my head, I rocked back and delivered a pitch.. Snap! It pops into the catcher's mitt. The words, "Strike!" and "Yeah!" explode from the ump and Assistant Coach Fowler, simultaneously. "Hmm," comes to mind. The pitch went directly into the center of the mitt. He did not move it an inch. I received the ball. I walked around to the back of the mound calming the storm in my head. I have to make another go of it. I breathe, slow in and all the way out. I toe the mound and lean forward to receive the sign. Again, it is held front and center. Everyone knows what I am throwing. Nothing cute. It is not about trickery or making the perfect pitch. 'Just throw one over.' Another calming breath and I rock back and let loose another pitch. Snap! "Strike!"

"Yeah!" This time Sam and a few others join Coach Fowler's bellow. Two pitches, two strikes, no swings. The take sign was on. No doubt. I hadn't thought about the take sign, but along with everybody else in attendance, it was clear to me a walk would do the job. Starting with two balls, it was the odds on favorite to be the outcome. Now the take sign would be off, but I had gained two more warm-up pitches and confidence from seeing the ball explode into the glove without the catcher moving it one iota. My release point was spot on. I position myself on the mound. I breathe and hold the ball in my glove with my right hand over it, grasping the ball with my standard two-seam fastball grip as I take the sign. Nothing has changed. Mark is calling for a waist high fastball. I give a slow nod, rock back, pivot on my right foot, stretch my left leg towards home plate, and with a whoosh of the bat, the ball snaps into the mitt. "Strike three!" "Yeah!!" Now the whole bench is into it. And my confidence is solid. I feel totally secure. Coach Stafford put the game in perspective, now I am riding the wave that Coach Fowler has formed and the rest are adding on. Mark did not have to move his mitt a millimeter for any of the first three pitches and that first batter was out after a token weak, late swing.

There is generally some chatter during a baseball game and some occasional shouts, but my pitches were eliciting roars from our bench. I say bench, but no one was on the bench. Everyone was standing at the front edge of the dugout and engaged with this inning. This game was beginning to look a little less like a wasted opportunity and more like a chance for something special The next batter took his place in the box. Mark and I went through the same ritual, I stepped on the mound and looked in, and he deliberately called for a fastball. Now it was less of a wakeup call to me and more a call to throw another fire ball that they cannot touch. I had a little bit of nerves delivering this pitch, but when it met the glove with a pop, I was over my emotions for good. It is one thing to have nerves and an altogether different thing to give in to them. I threw gas two more times, and he went to the dugout after three pitches had slammed into Mark's glove. The bench was ecstatic. Jubilant. And after every pitch, they all cheered, none louder than Coach Fowler and Sam.

The situation, so dire before, so different now. Bases loaded. Two out. We are up by one. In my changed mental framework the runners barely existed anymore. "It is me and you," I confide in some spiritual plane to the batter. I am not sure I ever in my life broke 70 miles per hour, but if I did, it was that day. I was fully loose by the time I struck out the first guy. And after six straight fastballs, I was letting it rip and the ball had a little something more on it than normal. I felt the excitement and the adrenaline of the moment, but there was a little something extra. That was evident, when I fired the next ball. Again I rocked back and sent one rocketing directly towards home plate. This time the batter was going for a first pitch hit, maybe hoping to be aggressive and catch me off guard. His swing produced a slow rolling grounder in the direction of first base. I ran to it, calmly fielded the ball and tossed it to the first baseman who squeezed the third and final out of the inning. Our bench went nuts. What the heck had I just pulled off? It had taken 14 pitches to create the mess and seven to redeem it. I returned to a dugout of handshakes, high fives, and back slaps starting with Coach Stafford, followed by Sam, Coach Fowler and the rest of my teammates.

That inning. Those seven pitches. Those shouts. That was the moment. It wasn't just baseball; it was something else. It was revelation that the impossible is possible if you give yourself a chance. We forget that. Life has it's ups and downs, but it has a lot of sideways too. Moments where what is supposed to happen, habitually does. Moments this spectacular come along so rarely that we can lose sight of the possibility of the truly miraculous, through our over exposure to the norm and mundane.

I would have to return to the mound for the seventh inning and preserve the win for Sam. I was credited with a hard fought save. The sixth I remember in such clear detail. I know well enough about the seventh, and it was important for preserving what was accomplished the inning prior. Had I conceded the winning or even tying run in the bottom of the last, the triumph of the sixth would have been a moment instead of an event that lives in me. There was something to those pitches, that inning, the words from coach, the sign and glove of Mark, the seven strikes, the three outs and the shouts from our dugout. There was a timeless magic, a substance present. We witnessed the impossible. As I was called into the center of the worst competitive calamity imaginable, I was also at the heart of overcoming it.

The hill can be a lonely place, but it wasn't that day at Kimble Stadium. The sound of a ball popping into a catcher's mitt took on a whole new meaning that day. When I am at a game and I hear that sound, it draws me back to that day. Through all the chaos, there was an intimate and surreal connection with my coaches, Mark and the rest of our team. Not to be too dramatic, but that moment represented something greater than what I alone could have done. We all witnessed something bigger than all the training in the world could have produced. It was a magic moment, and that inning testified to what greatness can happen in a circumstance if only we have the guts to let it.

Why Adversity? What is the Purpose of Competition?

I am noticing as an adult, that there are still some things that are a struggle. Sometimes, it is a little like having that posse chasing me around and around the playground. It never quite overcomes me, but it never lets me out of its range either. It is just there. I want to out-run it and out last it, but I can't. Maybe you know the feeling?

I know in my thinking, I get overwhelmed because I see all that is in front of me. There are a few things that wear me out a little. The things still on my to do list. And some days, I don't know if I have what it takes to stop running and turn and face all these issues at once. If I work on one area, it seems to make the other problems loom larger. The instant I say I am going to fix something is the moment it becomes harder. Have you ever been here? I think the Apostle Paul wrote about this or a similar struggle in Romans 7. Perhaps what adversity does, is test how resolute we are. Because it is easy to feign resolve, it is only proper that our stance is tested. I wonder if outsiders can sense the whole mob swirling around. Maybe they can just see Fred, the issue that is supposed to be confronted, right now. You see, like on the playground, there is only one heavyweight bout on the card. Regardless of how many are in attendance, the others are mere spectators. And no matter how intimidated you are, you will have to face it eventually. It's time to notice the fatigue in your legs and the tiredness of your chest.

Begin to gather yourself. Begin to own your life and surroundings. Look, you may be surrounded, but there is one person, one issue you are encountering. Stop looking at everything and concentrate on what is pushed up right in front of you. Even though there were 11 boys in the mob, nine were nobodies. It came down to two, the boy I had to face and the one ring leader who would make sure I did. If I were to put two faces to most problems, the first would be the fear of failure, and the second would be the fear of success. The fear of or facing failure makes us avoid things. It is like not wanting to face the kid with the reputation for beating people up because you are afraid you will get mangled. And it is the fear of showing your face to your parents if it has been bruised a little. The thing about this is your parents have your back whenever you experience difficulty. In life as in sports, they are your biggest supporters, and though they want all to be well always, they really are there for you, through the thick and thin.

The fear of success sounds a little like this, "If I overcome this, then I can't use that excuse anymore, I will have to be that other person. If I lose the weight, then I can't go crazy and overindulge anymore. If I stop using, then I can't be free and do what I want anymore. If I throw away the credit cards, then I can't get the stuff I want any time I feel like it. If I grow up, then I can't act like a child anymore." This is hitting home a little bit right now. The fear of success also sounds very different, "People will notice me and think I am special. I am not special, I have so many failures compared to successes. I don't want to live a lie that I am perfect. I don't want to embarrass somebody else. I just want to blend in." It is one thing to be superior and successful at something, and intentionally hold back for the gain of someone else. It is entirely different to let uncontrolled thoughts sabotage your abilities and cause you to not reach your potential.

I want to rephrase this one more way: There is one issue, one monster you have to face, and then there is your life and your circumstances that will make sure you face it. You will get to a point of fatigue and you will just say, 'It's now or never,' which is a great place to be. Through this process glory will come in. You will wear the mantle of success and keep it. When I eventually stopped and faced Fred, I committed to doing it and seeing it through to the end. I faced him without the weakening effects of fear. Committed means I was 100% in. And the funny thing is, the battle was over in less than a minute. And the second time we grappled it took only an instant and we never battled again. What a powerful image to center our hope around.

I am not a person that advocates living your life trying to win everything you compete in, badminton for instance, but there are some battles you are equipped to win. There are some battles you want to win. And there are some battles you have to win. And then there are some battles you will find joy seeing the other guy win (especially when you have kids). Remember after a contest, win or lose, to be a good sport and shake hands. If you have a bout of words with your spouse, kiss and make up. Or if the contention is with another loved one, co-worker or friend, reconcile. It is not unhealthy to disagree, you just need to be sure the relationship is a priority and there is no lingering pain or separation. It is not our problems that wear us down, it is not confronting and resolving them that is such a drain.

At the end of the altercation, regardless of the cause, for recreation or for reason, there is an awesome, inherent opportunity for bonding. Fred and I were friends a long time after our encounter. Not best friends, but there was mutual respect present. Also, I said before that Sam gave me a look of satisfaction after I had bested his title holder in the wrestling match. Maybe he knew something that I didn't, that a moment like that would change my life. He knew that when I remembered to be, I proved to myself that I was a fighter. I proved to myself that I could face intimidation. I proved to myself that I was able, even if not willing to initiate, but certainly able, to push past adversity and settle into victory. Maybe I am giving Sam too much credit and he was just thinking ahead to a rematch, either way, the satisfaction on his face was clear and genuine.

Every time in my life that I have been brought into a must win situation and faced it and gained a victory, I have experienced power. And though it should have had a greater impact on my character, at minimum, it revealed to the others who witnessed and to me, glory. What do I mean by glory? It is that little something extra. It can't be rationalized only experienced and witnessed. I prefer nine times out of ten to play competition I am equal to or slightly better than. Both sides feel pretty good about themselves, they both have a measure of success and maybe find more room to grow in the end. But that one other time, that tenth time, I want to face Goliath. I want to take down the giant. If taking down that giant is a win, then great. At the end of the game, win or lose, he has to know he was stood up to with everything you got. I really am not one to let the scoreboard tell me if I am a winner or a loser. When I face my opponent full out, I win.

As a youth sports coach, it can be tough to rally kids to face a team that is exceptional, or if they have a kid that is an extra foot taller or someone that is just super talented. Kids are smart and care about being successful. So what do you tell them, 'Hey you are going to get whipped tonight, but play hard anyway.' 'Maybe this will be the night you get real lucky.' When that team makes a run on them, scores easy and puts so much pressure on that your team loses the ball, it can rattle them. Kids can let the first few minutes or even pre-game handshakes mess up what they do well. I believe intimidation causes scores to be more lopsided than they would otherwise be. Youth athletes have to learn and develop nerve. They have to know they are going to take some punches and still be able to stand. Then they will take a few more. Then they have to learn to deliver some punches of their own. They have what it takes, they just have to believe in themselves. Bring on Goliath. We can live with the results, I just want to see if we can knock him down to life size.

A basketball team I recently coached made it through the season undefeated. One team they played three times had very little experience and the scores were pretty lopsided. This group of boys I was coaching had never experienced winning by a large margin before. Nor had I as a coach. It posed a new challenge, make the game a learning experience and keep the team competing. In my opinion, at the level of competition we are in, it wouldn't really benefit anyone to win by 40. So we adjusted our defense and moved some players into positions they don't get to play all that often. A second team we only played one time. It was a back and forth game. Both teams played incredibly well. It was great to see my team continue to dig deep and to finish the game with their best quarter and a win. It was a total war. The third team on our schedule, we had the privilege to compete against four times. They were our number one rival and every game was decided by a basket or less. Two games ended in wins and two ties. To watch both teams go out there during each contest and battle it out from start to finish and one basket decide the game was incredible. Each meeting, both sets of players elevated their game. They competed even harder and with more focus. The margin for making a pass, dribbling to the basket or taking an open shot tightened. All the kids involved showed tremendous guts and were the better for having these four opportunities. Great gratitude and respect developed over the four meetings. The two teams competed all out with awesome sportsmanship.

Scrimmaging is a great way to give a team experience beyond working on individual skills and plays, but it isn't the real thing. The kids know the difference. It is something about showing up to the gym and seeing an unfamiliar team with different colored shirts that makes it worth giving your all. On game day there is a whole new level of intensity. Watching kids learn how to scrap, to invest themselves in overcoming and believing in themselves is worth the time put in. It is the ultimate reward. We need to be ready to take on that fierceness, intensity and resolute attitude in our every day lives. Our real life is not a scrimmage. And it is not just filled with the easy battles, or even ones, but with ones we don't know if we can win. We have to keep up the fight and endure, even those very challenging conflicts can be added to the win column or at least decided in a draw.

So what are the games for? Winning? Being the best? Having fun? That is a part of it, especially having fun. But the bigger part of competition is designed for you to grow and find new levels of leadership and functionality. It is fierce and friendly. More fierce during, and more friendly immediately after the clock ticks to zero. We put on different colored uniforms to bring out the best in each other, not to thwart. Somehow that sense of foreignness draws out your greatest ability. You set your sights at winning, but the hidden benefit is growth and maturity.

In my own youth, playing against a baseball team that moved their outfielders back invited me to hit the ball farther. And I did. Each time they moved a few more steps back, I answered by hitting it that much farther. My favorite bat was profoundly dented from slamming it into the ball so many times, but I kept answering the call to be better. And the call came from the opposition. Your job as an athlete isn't to ruin their day, but rather, it is to produce and to invite them to answer, while making it absolutely as difficult as possible for them to answer. That is it in a nut shell. You are not really thinking of it at the time, but essentially, competition's purpose is to eliminate weakness from each other. If a person has the passion and drive to succeed and become their absolute best, they cannot really view their rivals as the enemy, but instead in an abstract way, as their ally. Let me say this again, if your goal is personal development and overcoming adversity, then does not the opposition encourage and stimulate the growth you are looking to achieve? It is the nemesis you encounter over and over that drives you to work harder. So be thankful not bitter towards the kids in the other shirts. That goes for parents, coaches and players.

As a team, approach the game with fierceness, focus, preparedness, intensity and the desire to compete. And after you have competed with all your might, realize the gift each team has offered the other in turn. You want to begin each week of practice with the mindset, 'I have to get better because I know how hard the other team prepares.' And, 'I don't want their job to be easy next time; I want them to have to work for every point and every defensive stop.' Do not dare to have a bad week of practice or to go out and play a sub par game because of the disservice it is to you and the other team.

I don't know how many think of it this way, but in the place of struggle, whether it is in sports against a team that has had your number, against another business that competes with you for market share, with a personal issue that has you frustrated, whatever the case, the struggle doesn't have to be a negative, but can quickly be viewed as an opportunity for success. If you have been knocked around a little by this opposition, then start with the acknowledgement of the earlier defeats and begin to be thankful that you might actually overcome the foe. Think about what it will mean to achieve this victory. And moment by moment take steps of success to overcome without giving in to frustration and feelings of defeat, regardless of the outcome of your effort from a moment ago and the current circumstance. Just keep picking up from here. Take one positive step forward at a time, forget about what was and don't worry about what will be. Focus on and work through the now and that will change both what is possible and what has already happened. Work to stack up success here. Now. And what ever you do, don't fear failure. When you fear failure, you hold back from giving your all. Failure is normal. It is part of the process to success. The opposition scores points too, try to limit the amount of times the adversary gets a point and keep trying to score points of your own. That's all there is to it. Acknowledge and understand the goal you are trying to defend and also visualize the path to scoring.

You are always going to have competition. Some friendly, some not. There will always be an obstacle to overcome. Get excited about it. Golf maybe gives the purest perspective into the real source of competition. The field, leader board and the course establish the situation and context through which the individual athlete applies himself. The weakness within is the real opponent. A bad backswing or follow through, a mental lapse, a misread, a bad break all can take you from the plush green grass into a hazard faster than you can say 'Fore!' If not careful, that one mistake can lead to a total meltdown. So we just consider the circumstance we are in, prepare for the next shot, take the next shot and then deal with the circumstances it leaves us in and repeat.

Leadership

From my personal perspective, leadership may be one of the most challenging facets of sports and perhaps life in general. It seems that coaches and society want to or need to narrow down the field to two or three leaders, captains, supervisors, for every group of ten to fifteen others. This is a perfectly sensible way of administrating and some individuals tend to respond better to their peers. However, if a dynamic develops, because of a poor understanding or demonstration of leadership, where the one or two are directing traffic and the others are waiting for direction, approval and permission to excel and move outside their existing productivity boundaries; instead of a net gain, you can end up with a net loss. What can also be lost is the knowledge that can only be gained at the front line, not making it's way back to the parties responsible for corporate decision-making or the experience of those decision makers not being dispersed to the masses. That's not to say you cannot have captains or an inner circle, and having appropriate boundaries of authority is very positive when understood and maintained. You just have to call out every ounce of leadership from every member you have on your team and help them develop self-confidence.

You can see good or poor examples of leadership in any type of system, whether it is a team, work place, church, government body etc. Leadership in it's greatest form isn't taking over and encouraging others to let you. It isn't about dominating those on your own squad, although I have seen that often enough. It isn't a pecking order. Nope. That's not it.

The root of leadership is actually inclusive. It is about pulling more in, not pushing others away. It is about playing to your fullest and encouraging others to do the same, through your attitude, words and actions. It is about contributing what you have and letting those around you know they can't get away with letting you do all the work. There is no doubt players have to be ready to step up and take over offensively and/or defensively at different parts of a game. That is leadership and a beautiful aspect of sports, too. But the other guys have to stay involved. And you really cannot set out to play that way for a whole game and a whole season, because eventually you will go against a higher level of competition and be defeated because you did not develop the other players. If someone is having an off shooting performance, he can find other ways to contribute and stay involved, but also has to be ready to shoot. When the ball comes to you in the rotation and you have the open look, it is your turn, take the shot. Each at bat you have to be prepared and confident you will make good contact. Another word on the matter, if a player is talented enough to take over and dominate, he should also be able to make other players around him better and involve them.

Watching a point guard come down and get his shot and score some baskets to give his team a boost has a different look than a point guard not involving his team. I have had the good fortune to coach a young man, that at our level of competition, he was the best player on the court every game, but he did not take his teammates for granted. He is blessed with amazing maturity, and as the team's point guard, he seeks to distribute the ball and treats each player equally. He puts trust in them and continues to go to the open player, and they in turn take quality shots, sometimes making and sometimes not. He also gets open shots for himself. The point guard I am referring to only takes over as needed to correct a scoreless trend, stop a run by the other team, or set a tone and give a moral boost to his team. He is ultra competitive and highly inclusive at the same time. It is remarkable to watch a young man play the right way. He is treating all five players on the court, including himself, as valued members.

I point that out because kids play better when they feel included, and they give more. Someone who doesn't feel included holds back, protects himself, doesn't commit. Each player on the court or field is responsible for scoring. Even when they do not have possession of the ball, even in a situation where they are part of the defensive unit. Each player in the game is part of transitioning from defense to offense and the process of producing a score. A player works hard on defense to force a turnover or get a rebound and that is the first step to your team scoring. In baseball it is the third out that transitions your team to offense.

A bit off the subject, but worth using as an example, my best friend growing up was naturally the center of attention socially. While it was normal for me to step into the spotlight in athletics and academics, I also found a way of offering my comedic side among my peers. I could always find my comfort zone around this friend and I was willing to join him in the social spotlight. It was always big enough for the both of us (and others). And as we matured, we invested our talents in various athletic, social and academic activities, always trying to set high standards in each.

When I married my college sweetheart, I now was paired with the most amazing person I knew. I was so awed by her, that I began to allow her to gain the spotlight by herself, and in fact, I encouraged her to take it. I fell back and just allowed her amazing entertainment skills to carry conversations we were having as a couple. Her stories were always far more interesting and her delivery was incredible. She was a natural comedian and social superstar. But so was my school chum. So why was I now shrinking back? Why did I stop challenging myself and offering myself? I was never intimidated by my best friend, but with my wife, for a time, I began to see myself as a bit inadequate. I became more of a spectator before finally realizing I had to contribute too. That is an important revelation for us to have no matter what the arena. 'I need to contribute too.' The situations of sports and life produce opportunities for us to share our talents, to reveal and share ourselves. Essentially the point is, 'I need to do my part.'

A superstar like a Jordan, Kobe, Lebron... can come through at any point in the game, but they are best when they bring out the skills in everyone around them too. I think it takes a special person to grow and become their personal best when there is a player of that magnitude. I have seen very good players take over and make their teammates feel/look/act like also rans. When a player is succeeding, the team is succeeding; so it is just a matter of doing so in the context of a team. As mentioned before, I have also seen the best player on the court concentrate on bringing other players into the mix and giving them the opportunity to succeed or fail. To be able to make that differentiation at any age is a credit, and a true gift when it comes at an early age, when the kids around them may not know how to initiate or participate.

An example of a person's potential impact, and not just waiting for the right opportunity to come his way, is the accomplishments of Nelson Mandela. His work that would eventually eliminate a tragic sociopolitical system and heal a country began from a prison. While his political stances and activity began before and, in fact, were the cause of his imprisonment, he and those he partnered with began to transition South Africa out of the system of apartheid through a span of decades. On more than one occasion, he was offered release from prison if he agreed to certain concessions that would have hurt the cause he stood for. He refused such offers. What if he did not continue with his cause and assert himself while in prison? Answer, he would not have lived to see blacks, the populous majority in South Africa, vote. And he would not have been elected President of South Africa just four years after agreeing to acceptable terms for release from prison, in which he served 27 years of a life sentence as a political prisoner.

Leadership is being pointed in the right direction and taking action. It does not need to have the most glamorous platform. You don't need the loudest voice or even the most followers or in some circumstances any followers. You offer the contribution you are capable of giving. All of it. You just keep doing the right thing and expressing yourself and your talents.

Leadership is innovative. Bring a new skill to the team. Learn how to bunt or turn a double play. Be the one who does the dirty work of setting screens. Perfect the give and go by working a little extra after practice. Go to an extra, voluntary camp. Train to be faster and stronger. You offer yourself. You learn a skill and you offer it to the team for others to learn. You show self-control and help produce a learning environment. You hustle.

It's about participation. Offering yourself. Your whole self. Just running up and down the field or standing by a base is not participation. The goal is to give your full attention, your mind, body and spirit all working to the same ends. Some of the younger boys seem as though they have a disconnect between their minds and bodies, or at least a lack of commitment to the activity they are involved in. They want to sign up for a sport and like it, but would rather think about or converse about something else while there. However, if they keep coming and begin to work and see some positive results, they slowly let go of the distractions and begin giving themselves to the sport.

You can't just follow along. You have to initiate. If you follow along, you allow someone else to be master and you don't bring the full amount of success. Leadership makes decisions. Good decisions. It learns from and prunes off bad decisions. It notices the results of their actions and the tendencies of others.

'If you know it. Show it.' That is something I like to say. I really don't care too much about what someone knows. It is what they are willing to show that gets it done. You can know everything and keep it bottled up inside, I say this from my experience too. It is what you express through your body that the rest of the world can enjoy too.

You have to evaluate the situation, look for opportunities and respond with your genuine talents and contribute. Trade in the bad habit of waiting for the good habit of looking. In soccer a kid's mind might be set to wait for the ball to come to him and then act, start dribbling or try to score or pass. Instead of waiting and giving the game and the other players the responsibility to involve you, *look* to get involved. *Look* to step in front of a pass and make a steal. *Look* for a lane that is open to receive a pass and move into it. Go win a ball. Charge hard to the goal and *look* for a rebound.

Leadership is individual but not singular. It may be up to the individual to offer it, but what you really want is a team of leaders cooperating. We each have a style and skill set that is unique for us to offer. And if we don't offer it, the team misses out. In sport and out of sport, you have your set of skills that you are expert, secure, developing or that are buried. And life is about unearthing, applying and sharing those talents.

Being a leader is being pointed in the right direction and bringing action. It is weeding out bad ideas as they come and developing newer more mature levels of response. One way to stay pointed in the right direction is to *Know the Situation.* This is also preparedness. In baseball it sounds like this. 1 out, a ball and two strikes on the batter, a runner on first and third, the game is tied 2 to 2 in the bottom of the fourth with Johnny up to bat. Or 1 down, the batter is behind in the count 1 and 2, there are 2 ducks on the pond (or runners at the corners). For football, know the score, down and distance, and how much time is left. You can practice this stuff when the game is on the television or you are on the sidelines. Don't just stare and wait to see what happens, think about the setting, the circumstance the players are in. It really matters. And also, use your words in a constructive way. Knowing the situation and reading the play go hand-in-hand. And now that you are aware of the circumstance, be ready. Anticipate. Act immediately, without hesitation. You've prepared for this moment. It is about bringing your contribution. Whatever it is.

There are regular and obvious skills to learn, but what about the abstract. How about learning to adjust your attitude, choose to have motivation and a competitive spirit. Identify what opportunities are available, decide which ones you can be successful at and go no holds barred to make it happen.

Leadership summary:

1. **An *individuals unique contribution*.** Talent is a gift to you, and a contribution is showing the understanding that you have a gift and putting it in play for the sake of yourself and those around you.

2. **Know the situation.** Take a moment and become aware of the situation. It will help you to anticipate and make the proper response faster.

3. **Involve others.** This may be a challenge for some to learn, but you are a much greater leader when you get contribution from others.

4. **Be a role model.** Whether it is sports, school, the office or home, just show up every day and do your job regardless how thankless it might be.

5. **Direction and action.** You are not leading if you are going in the wrong direction. You are just getting yourself and whoever is with you further behind. And being pointed in the right direction without movement is not getting it done either. Check your direction and start marching.

6. **Communicate.** Communication is both listening and speaking. Do both. Be a great listener and speak up. Communicating on the ball diamond, the court or field keeps your mind and body ready for action and integrated with the team aspect of the game.

7. **Innovation.** Keep bringing new, positive innovation to the team, office, school and home. Being exceptional at a skill is great. Adding to skills and becoming more diverse, while maintaining and increasing areas of expertise is even better. The race isn't over. Keep growing, those around you will benefit. They will snatch up those innovations and grow too.

8. **Motivation and commitment.** When motivated or inspired, we can do amazing things. And being committed to something helps you to focus and invest in that endeavor. So why not explore healthy ways to commit to being motivated.

9. **Confidence.** This can make or break you. If you are confident, you are rock solid. If unsure or overconfident, you lose your strength.

10. **Attitude.** Learning that you can decide what attitude

you have towards an event is an amazing lesson. Practice it! Your attitude is the straw that stirs the drink and maybe the hugest success factor, even above talent. Put on kindness, patience, forgiveness, willingness, hope, effort, determination, endurance and a team perspective. It will get you farther. Have the attitude to adopt and grow in as many of these leadership qualities as possible. Remain committed and be understanding when some come as a challenge. Setting the right attitude even helps with eating your vegetables and doing your chores.

Learning to Win

Winning in the head-to-head competition of sports, in the office, in the home and more abstractly within self has many ways for keeping score. Regardless of the measurement of success, success and winning is no accident. It is worked for and earned. Winning is prepared for and harvested like a farmer plants his field to receive a yield later on in the year. And with the most talented individuals, responsibility is a companion to winning. Winning is a process.

My son's baseball team decided to play up last fall. Instead of staying in coach pitch with kids their age, they signed up for kid pitch and played with kids a year older. At his age, a year is a lot, not to mention there would not be a parent trying to pitch where they were swinging. Now, there was a more mature ball player trying to get the ball past them. The strike zone was huge and the pitches were much more random. Some of the pitchers they faced had some impressive velocity. The kids got in there and faced them regardless of how fast they could chuck the ball. Their courage was tested most when the kid right in front of them got hit by a pitch. There were more than a few rib shots and batters that were brought to tears. But they kept going out there one after another and taking their turn. They paid their dues and grew. I think this was pretty tough at times for the parents to witness, but I am sure everyone had a sense of pride at witnessing the toughness and resolve their youngsters showed.

A few keys to winning:

1. Love the game. Every accomplishment I had on the baseball diamond, including pitching out of the most desperate of situations, was born out of my love for the game. I woke up every day of my childhood ready to play baseball, kickball, wiffleball, home run derby, pitch to my dad, play catch, any and all of it. It wasn't a burden to train to be a baseball player; it was what I most wanted to do.

2. Learn the game. Don't take it for granted that you know everything. There is a depth to sports and always something new you can learn so you can bring innovation to your game. Understand the phases of the game, offense, defense, transition and find out what makes them work. Here are some basics:

The purpose of offense is to accumulate points. In baseball you hit the ball where the fielders are not, advancing the runners from base to base and across the plate. In basketball, soccer, hockey and football you control and protect the ball and advance it towards the opponents goal. In football, the job of the offensive lineman is to move the man in front of him. For the home, you go to work, apply yourself, use your talents and earn an income.

The purpose of defense is to transition to offense without giving up points. This is a team goal. How does this get done? Let's break down the general concept of defense for some sports. Baseball, you defend the bases and the dimensions of the field attempting to gain three outs before batters advance around the bases to score. Basketball, you pressure the ball handler, take away the passing lanes, get to and secure the loose ball, defend the goal and rebound with intensity. You play the ball and defend the goal as a team. Soccer is very similar except how the players are distributed across the field and there is a player assigned full time to defending the goal. As for football's goal line defense, you don't give ground. Defend that line. At home, the check book may be what you are defending. You decide against that unnecessary purchase. You wait an extra month and pay cash for a good quality item that is needed. You transition from defense (the weekend) back to offense (the office) without giving up points (spending the cash you labored for last week).

3. Prepare for the game. Turn your passion for the game into developing yourself as a player. Show up to practice with the right attitude, which is... you are there to learn and develop your game. Get stronger. Stretch yourself. Become a student of the game; you need to grow your sports I.Q. to perform better. Watch your sport on t.v. a little, read about it, talk about your sport and your performances with a parent and study the details behind what makes a play successful or not. Train your body to be stronger and faster and more able to do the skills needed to play. Put in the extra work, take advantage of the opportunities available and invest in yourself. Go to an extra training session, sign up for a team or individual skills camp. Take care of yourself. Eat well. Sleep well. Make healthy decisions.

4. Respect the game. Be humble and thankful for every opportunity. The more humble you are, the greater your stature can become. We shouldn't take anything for granted, nor should we think we are entitled. Playing sports is a privilege. Be a model citizen on and off the field, plus get good grades. Listen to your coach and show

respect to your parents. Play with integrity. Show respect to the opposition, teammates and officials. Be a player of great character.

5. Enjoy the game. Sports are so unscripted. You don't know the outcome. That is part of the excitement. Another part is, you have been given a wonderful mind and body, and it is awesome to see what amazing things you can do. It is fun to challenge yourself. Also you get to develop friendships and spend time with a great group of guys. Because of the time the players have in the dugout, baseball is a great bonding sport. The players have a load of fun passing the time and cheering on their friends. We should bring that fun and bonding into all aspects of life.

6. Be a good sport and respect your opponent. Those other guys are trying their best too. You may finish the game with the most or the fewest points, but always try to appreciate the experience and the guys you had the opportunity to go to battle with and against. If you just think about the score, you'll miss the good stuff like personal growth, teamwork, friendship, community and the joy of playing.

7. Have a good team that you can count on. The guys

that wear the same uniform are on your team, but it goes beyond that. You may have a swing coach, a throwing mechanics coach, you may like to go to the same sporting goods supplier and of course your friends and family. Be invested in these relationships. Even those who compete in individual sports need to build a team around them. Having those people to share in your successes, to love and thank for driving you around, supporting you and investing in you is a great reward.

8. Have guts. Just get out there and play. Do what you can. Be fearless. Participate. Throw your hat in the ring and see what happens. See yourself as a valuable part of the group. Keep going no matter what. Work hard and play hard. Play life with a smile on your face; it might not look like it, but you could be a moment away from your greatest inning ever.

Reflection

I have had this memory of pitching at Kimble Stadium since I was 17. I decided to write The Greatest Inning Ever Pitched, because I thought it was a good story that would be well worth sharing if I could capture some of the magic of that day and give a quality back-story. As I began this project, I entered wanting and expecting this story to be inspiring, because it has been a source of inspiration and power for me to draw on whenever I remember that day in detail. What I did not expect to gain is a new practical view and better understanding for myself of Jesus being called in for me, my family and all of mankind, so I will share my findings. Like many, I have been a Christian my whole life. And for me, at least, understanding on a fresher, more personal and deeper level the purpose Jesus served is so beneficial. Writing this story gives me a new way to rationally understand and wrap my head around and really visualize better what Jesus pulled off. I think life has often felt a lot like I am on the mound walking or beaning batter after batter, at the plate taking a ball in the ribs or I am inheriting somebody else's bad situation. Or maybe even there is that mob giving chase, closing in on me and wearing me down. According to New Testament scriptures from the

Bible, (refer to the Appendix to read these verses) like John 3:16-17, John 12:44-47, John 15:5, Galatians 3:13-14, Ephesians 2:4-10, Philippians 2:5-8, Colossians 3:1-4, we are beyond that part of the story and Jesus is finishing the game for us, has finished the game for us and will finish the game for us. We should be like the teammates in the dugout and be excited. We know about the crown of thorns and the beating He took. Believe it or not, that is Jesus delivering fastballs. He is throwing strikes and getting outs. Jesus on the cross is like the first of three outs: death, then resurrection and finally ascension. He got the save, and He is the little something extra.

If He really has come in for us to be the closer, then why do at least some of us, maybe all or most of us, still experience struggles. Why does it still feel like we are dealing the pitches and the balance of the game is still in question, but this time it is about to get out of hand. He may be the pitcher of record but we are involved too. Let me explain. When we are overly wired or sensitive to our everyday circumstances, we can lose the perception of connection with Christ and the knowledge that He has taken the hill for us, and we are no longer the pitcher of record. It is easy to forget, but Jesus does have it all under control, and when we remember and embrace our union with Him in the midst of the circumstance, we will get through our situation more peacefully. I guess the best way to look at it is, we can have the stress, fear and negativity I was experiencing when I first took the mound in the sixth inning at Kimble Stadium and see how that goes. The other option is more like what I experienced once the words Coach Stafford spoke to me sunk in and the pressure was lifted from me or my father's words that gave me the courage to take back the third grade snow pile. The results speak for themselves.

So then our life should be perfectly easy? This goes back to the main point of the prologue, there are things we are undecided about, things that we have not seen how He has taken the mound and finished out the game. We may have an overall understanding and experience of this, but we need to realize that it goes farther, into the specific areas of our lives. This book is filled with true stories that through the act of putting it down in writing, cast a shadow of metaphor over my life, causing me to understand it a little more. I am writing about my observations and interpretations from my life in the trenches because I am willing to share my own perceptions and take the time to write them down. The process of writing has brought new contemplations and discoveries to me, so I am sharing what I found in the context it was uncovered.

And for those not familiar with the gospel, Jesus was the fulfillment of the terms of justice and curse. He was and is the full payment for all of life's debts that man has accumulated in relationship with sin. In short He was and is the answer. The one and only remedy. In the Bible many of the stories where someone is 'on trial,' it is not to make account of their crimes or guilt but to reveal and testify to their innocence. That's why Daniel was put in with the lions, to say 'This is what an innocent life is like. It can't be touched even by lions.' And David, it wasn't his fight or his might, it was his innocence and trust in the Lord who had shown him glory before, so he would have confidence even enough to face a giant. And Jesus is the picture of innocence overcoming our hopelessness through grace.

Lord knows we have done some stuff, and have at some point in our life got lost and strayed from the path for a time, and yet we have innocence available to us. It is remarkable to know that we can experience and cherish innocence, the most precious state conceivable, through

Jesus who set us free. And like I had to not focus on the batter to keep from beaning him early on, or avoid thoughts about the evidence of my circumstance when the odds were stacked against me at Kimble Stadium, we have to take our focus off what the running record says about us and give ourselves a chance. Measuring ourselves against opposition or even against our past deeds only makes our knees buckle and us less likely to try today, which is the task at hand. Our true nature is good, the garbage of our lives is just response to unsavory influences of thought, memory and emotion that portrays itself as our identity. It is a lot easier to encounter innocence when first you remember that you are good. That goodness is from God and He has not recalled what He has endowed us with. It is easier to overcome something when you believe you can, so give it some thought. Recognize the reality of the situation.

It doesn't seem like people talk about God in conversation much. Maybe that is the way it is supposed to be, I don't know. It does seem strange though. Whether you believe or not, it seems like it would be an interesting question to ask, 'Why do you believe?' I guess at the root of the 'God silence,' is a general inability for people to communicate, to translate something that is personal, perceived mostly introspectively and unique to another person. Nobody but me is going to have my experiences, and it would be a hard thing to explain some times, Ok, maybe almost always. But other days when the memory of having the little something extra is fresh, it is like having Life bottled up inside, just waiting for someone to share it with.

Maybe I became a writer because I grew tired of waiting for people to ask me about my life. Or maybe it is because I have worked for years in a cubicle and yet feel I have important stuff to share given the means. I discovered over time that I have to share me. As in sports, each person is a contributor to the end goal, and we just have to not withhold what we are able to offer.

To answer my own question, the reason I believe is because my life has brought me through places that has made it impossible not to and the understanding gained by what I have encountered. My life has taken a very different course than I would have expected, but I am so appreciative of it. I am even grateful of the things that got in the way and waited for me to overcome. I may be fatigued by what is yet in front of me, but I have courage that I will get beyond that too. I will come to the point when I see there is no escaping the encounter, and I turn to face the issue at hand.

I am looking forward to the moments, rare as they may be sometimes, when I am paying less attention to me, and I am more aware of peace and rest. I will be looking for Jesus on the mound peering in to take the sign, taking a deep breath, rocking back and delivering a strike, in The Greatest Inning Ever Pitched. I am thankful for the people, the teammates, the Sams and Freds and Coach Staffords and Fowlers, even the Coach Johns and Gregs and certainly my parents too. I am thankful to my family and to all who have been, even for a moment, part of my life, part of this great inning I am watching and cheering, 'Yeah!'

Epilogue

This story evolved from sharing about a game that I remember from my high school years into telling some additional childhood stories and reflections I have had through the writing process. I guess I consider that people have real things going on in their lives and not everything works out perfectly the first time through. So being real and sharing the good with the bad can shine a light of truth on life. I could have shared many mistakes in detail, but I only deem it helpful to point out glimpses to show the humanity that is present.

This book has a lot to do with coaching, but I want to also recognize the youth sports organizations, the refs, umpires and parents for setting aside time to drive their children to practices and games, bringing snacks and buying equipment, and playing in the yard, rink or driveway with their sons and daughters. It is such a joyful thing for kids to participate in sports, and there are a lot of wonderful people behind making it happen.

The main reason for writing this short piece is to inspire and communicate to readers, to give your all when called on. Never hold back and never give up. Just do your part, whatever it is, to your maximum ability. If something did not go perfectly yesterday, remember today is a new day and the past has no hold on it. If something did not go right 5 minutes ago, let it go. Learn and move on. We can go through times when we are showing great promise and other times of struggle. But through believing in the goodness and talents we have within and the source of these gifts, we can persevere with a little searching and some hard work. As long as we are still on the roster, we are never out of this game. Most of what we do, does not seem super glamorous. But regardless of our position we have a job to do. And the thing is, what we do is important. It is all those little things, the daily events and duties, that make up our life and our life is precious.

Appendix
(From the English Standard Version)

The Gospel of John 3:16-17

16 "For God so loved the world, that he gave his only Son, that whoever believes in him should not perish but have eternal life. 17 For God did not send his Son into the world to condemn the world, but in order that the world might be saved through him." Jesus of Nazareth

The Gospel of John 12:44-47

44 And Jesus cried out and said, "Whoever believes in me, believes not in me but in him who sent me. 45 And whoever sees me sees him who sent me. 46 I have come into the world as light, so that whoever believes in me may not remain in darkness. 47 If anyone hears my words and does not keep them, I do not judge him; for I did not come to judge the world but to save the world.

The Gospel of John 15:5

5 I am the vine; you are the branches. Whoever abides in me and I in him, he it is that bears much fruit, for apart from me you can do nothing.

Galatians 3:13-14

13 Christ redeemed us from the curse of the law by becoming a curse for us—for it is written, "Cursed is everyone who is hanged on a tree"— 14so that in Christ Jesus the blessing of Abraham might come to the Gentiles, so that we might receive the promised Spirit through faith.

Ephesians 2:4-10

4 But God, being rich in mercy, because of the great love with which he loved us, 5 even when we were dead in our trespasses, made us alive together with Christ— by grace you have been saved— 6 and raised us up with him and seated us with him in the heavenly places in Christ Jesus, 7 so that in the coming ages he might show the immeasurable riches of his grace in kindness toward us in Christ Jesus. 8 For by grace you have been saved through faith. And this is not your own doing; it is the gift of God, 9 not a result of works, so that no one may boast. 10 For we are his workmanship, created in Christ Jesus for good works, which God prepared beforehand, that we should walk in them.

Philippians 2:5-8

5 Have this mind among yourselves, which is yours in Christ Jesus, 6 who, though he was in the form of God, did not count equality with God a thing to be grasped, 7 but made himself nothing, taking the form of a servant, being born in the likeness of men. 8 And being found in human form, he humbled himself by becoming obedient to the point of death, even death on a cross.

Colossians 3:1-4

1 If then you have been raised with Christ, seek the things that are above, where Christ is, seated at the right hand of God. 2 Set your minds on things that are above, not on things that are on earth. 3 For you have died, and your life is hidden with Christ in God. 4 When Christ who is your life appears, then you also will appear with him in glory.

CPSIA information can be obtained at www.ICGtesting.com
Printed in the USA
BVOW08s0246250614

357284BV00009B/124/P